x leaves a mark;
signs, sober and undefined,
defying presence.

I am here.

Image not Found, Performance, 2016
Production in collaboration with the mediation team of FRAC-PACA

Image not Found.
Performance. 2016

Movement and the human body itself are proposed here as a *choreographic intervention* that develops as a statement of purpose for this exhibition, a statement that simultaneously questions the typological framework of the museum. That is to say, movement-based mediation between physical actors helps give audiences an alternative perspective, a new or different pathway towards accessibility and understanding. However, this pathway remains undefined, unfolding through the physical space of the gallery by means of these mediating bodies that are instrumental to the conception of the artworks in the exhibition: the art only becomes itself when this choreographic intervention takes place. With this activation of the space, the public is confronted with the performativity of each object, which in a classical presentation stays invisible. The typological restaging – a melding of forms and genres – creates a sense of surprise around the work, raising questions about its notional relation to the museum space, to the performers, to its own status as an object, and thereby unleashes the countless possibilities of a mind endlessly creating ephemeral images and impressions contingent on an unfixed, fleeting moment.

Protocol
In order to experience the *Image Not Found* performance, please:

1. Reserve a time slot at the front desk
2. Understand that only between 10 and 15 people are allowed at a time
3. Respect that cameras, smartphones, bags, and jackets are forbidden
4. Acknowledge that visitors under 10 years of age are permitted only with the strict guidance of an adult
5. Leave all food or drinks outside (eating or drinking is not permitted)

At the time of the reservation, two mediators will come to escort visitors from the front desk and guide them to the floor where the performance takes place. These mediators will open two large doors in the exhibition space, giving access to the gallery's 'preparation room', normally used only to uncrate artworks and to prepare them for installation. In the middle of the room is a stand with red painted gloves. Each participant receives a pair of these gloves to put over their hands. Meanwhile a voice whispers the narrative of the colors *Blue, White* and *Red* that are hanging as models on a wall. The mediators call the service elevator and take the visitors up to the performance floor. There two additional mediators (A and B) are waiting behind a mirror-curtain to begin the performance...

The Chinese Gloves, 2007
Every participant gets a pair of with red paint covered gloves before entering the elevator

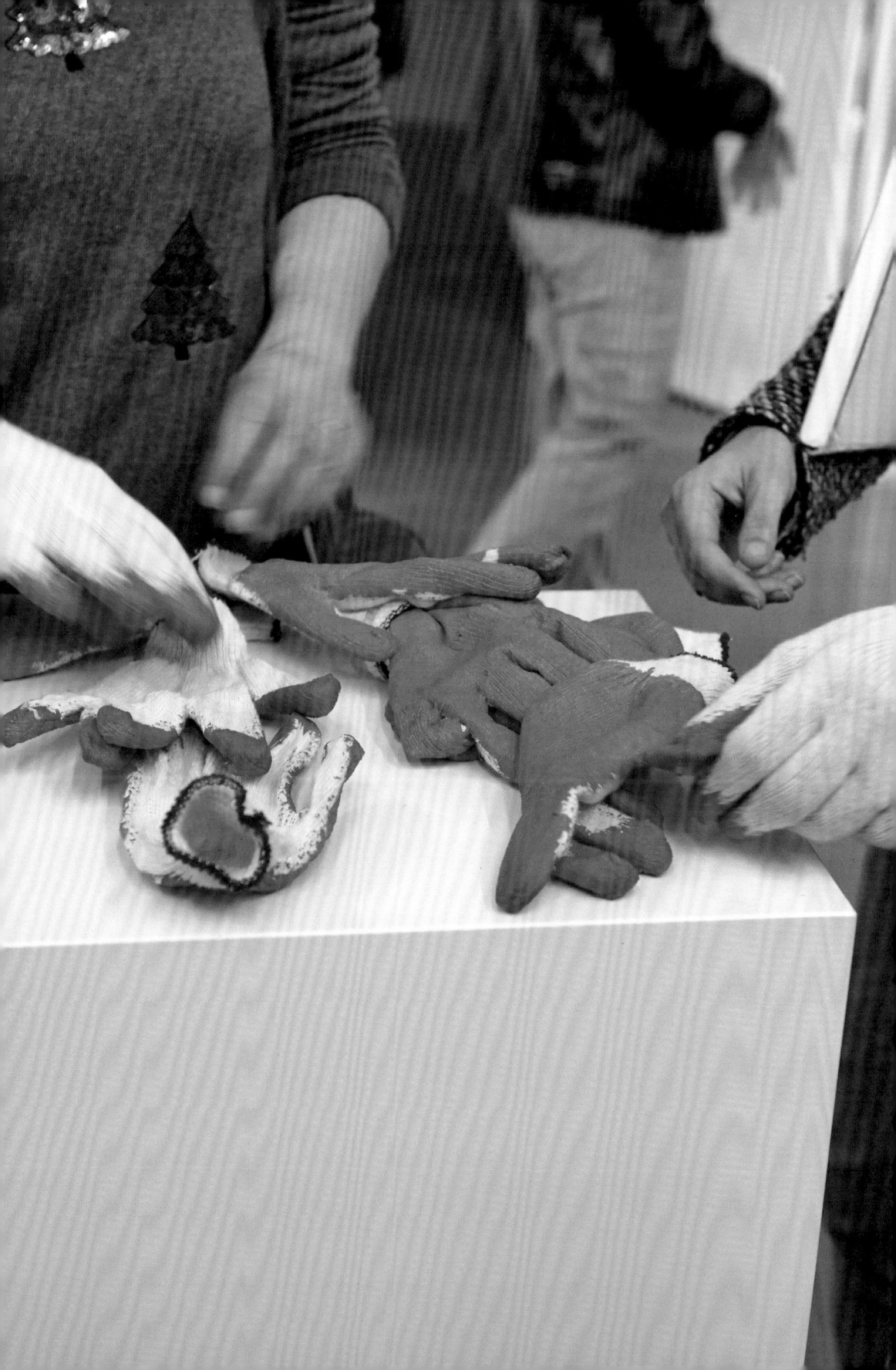

A: What do I see and what do we forget?

B: What do we know and what do we interpret?

A: We mediate the work, but the reality of meaning lies in your own interrelational presence between Object and Subject.

The Anonymous Letter.

Sir, Madam, or whoever you are, I gave the matter much thought before writing you this letter.
Son of an unknown father and uncertain mother and found on a wasteland, I, the not undersigned, was brought up by an anonymous benefactor.
I grew up in hiding in an unclear place. After completing some studies by correspondence in total solitude, I returned – with no identification or baggage, along a road, which is no longer on the map – to a place that I cannot reveal...
Once there, I wrote several anonymous letters to far-off correspondents... On the point of being discovered, I fled to the desert... where I am now writing to you from... You may be wondering why I am confiding in you when I don't even know you. It's nothing more than a moment of depression! As simple as that! There is no point trying to find out who I am – my name will mean nothing to you.

I sign off hesitantly,

The Abovementioned

A: A for Actor
   B for Bollywood
   C for Cinema
   D for Drama
   E for End
   F for Fame
   G for Gossip
   H for Hollywood
   I for Improvisation
   J for Jet-set
   K for Kitsch
   L for L.A.
   M for Movie
   N FOR NARCISSIST

B: Z for Zombie
   Y for Yoga
   X for X-rated
   W for Western
   V for Vanity
   U for U.S.
   T for Television
   S for Star
   R for Reality
   Q for Quiz
   P for Plot
   O for Oscar
   ...
   N FOR NARCISSIST

A: Every object is created through single
    elements that together build a whole.

B: Each individual piece builds a relation, which enables an object to exist in its full presence, in all its layers and fragilities.

A: Here we are, you and me.

B: Presence and absence in an interchangeable movement, never ending, always evolving.

A: We create and we deconstruct, but what persists is our own understanding of a limitless space between subject and object.

A: Beauty. It's a calculation, a wondering, an undefined existence.

B: No image can capture it, no meaning can define it.

A: It only persists in the fluid relations between perfection and default.

B: An untouchable state of mind.

A: The Sublime is the greatness beyond all boundaries, surpassing all possibility of calculation, measurement or imitation.

B: Beauty is the understanding of the sublime, but the sublime is an unmediated truth outside all definitions. It demarcates the possible travel of the mind to create one owns limitless ideas.

Tanguy Eeckhout

About the Tower of Babel, the lost image and the found object.
About the Tower of Babel, the lost image and the found object.
About the Tower of Babel, the lost image and the found object.
About the Tower of Babel, the lost image and the found object.
About the Tower of Babel, the lost image and the found object.
About the Tower of Babel, the lost image and the found object.
About the Tower of Babel, the lost image and the found object.
About the Tower of Babel, the lost image and the found object.
About the Tower of Babel, the lost image and the found object.

At the dawn of our civilisation, a tower would be erected that was meant to reach into the heavens. Earth was inhabited by a single people that, coerced by King Nimrod, unitedly undertook construction of this megalomaniac but doomed building. God, sensing a threat to his heavenly omnipotence, caused a general confusion of tongues among the building people, so they would no longer understand each other and their might would crumble and mankind would be scattered abroad over the face of all the earth. Since people could no longer understand each other and even the king's words were suddenly unintelligible and deprived of meaning, they all went their separate ways, in search of freedom. Perhaps imagination originated here in Babel, following the confusion of tongues. While previously, all had spoken the king's language, overnight, each had their own language and thus their own way of thinking and expressing themselves, which is essential to the development of imagination.

Lieven De Boeck could have been a citizen of Babel. His thinking is permeated by the paradox of life: the desire to be part of a larger whole and to fully experience one's individual freedom at the same time. Lieven De Boeck, who started his professional career as an architect, decided somewhere around 2002 that working with his own imagination was infinitely more challenging to him than building someone else's projects. As an artist you can strive for the unattainable and still be free to live out your wilfulness.

Lieven De Boeck's exhibition projects *Image Not Found* and *Objet Trouvé*, both realised in 2016, together made up the contemplation of an artistic practice spanning more than a decade. It was all but inevitable that the paradox would be deeply seated in both these projects. The exhibitions constitute a walk through an important ensemble of works and in both cases the exposition started with the piece *White Flags*. The concept of the white flags dates back to the inception of Lieven De Boeck's work: in 2002, he created a preliminary white flag as a proposal for a new European flag. A few years later, in 2006, he exhibited a first version of *White Flags* that was still made of paper. In 2010-2011, he hung out his white version of the Belgian flag on the front of his Brussels gallery for an entire year, and in 2014, he realised the nylon version of his *White Flags*. The 193 flags represent the contradiction between a united and a divided world but they also address the significance of a sign: the flag is a strong symbol with a clear meaning but once it is stripped of its colours, it becomes a subtle abstract composition of lines and shapes, peaceful and quiet, and it loses its univocal symbolic value. All this goes to show that the nucleus of his work already contained this play with sometimes minimal shifts in order to change social or political symbols into poetical signs.

Architecture, art and man form the triumvirate that largely determines the acts and thoughts of Lieven De Boeck. Architecture is the mould or form that encapsulates the artwork and man, while the artwork is man's 'imaginative object'. In other words: architecture shapes the performance of both the artwork and man and good architecture, therefore, is a mould inside of which imagination can unfold. Constructions like the Tower of Babel, on the other hand, are a mould for man's megalomania, barren and empty. For this reason the Tower of Babel, like Pieter Bruegel the Elder depicted it for the first time, is anything but harmonious and looks rather unstable in spite of its massive bulkiness. In Lieven De Boeck's world of imagination, universal principles of harmony like those of the golden mean and the Fibonacci sequence, converge with systems of measurement derived from the sizes and proportions of his own body. It is his way to manipulate all-embracing principles and provide them with new and personal meanings.

What is a work of art? Image or signification? What is an oeuvre? An archive of images or an accumulation of significations? In Lieven De Boeck's work images and meanings are disappearing all the time, as he once already indicated with the title *The Archive of Disappearance*. He disrupts the arbitrary connection between signifier and signified, creating his own signs and significations. That's why the image you are looking for has disappeared, while the object you found can only be interpreted within the artist's reason. In 2006, Lieven De Boeck already developed his own alphabet in New York, designing a new shape for each letter of the alphabet based upon the spray-painted tags he found in the streets of New York: it became an imagery-for-one that allowed him the freedom to use language and signs any way he liked in his personal sign system. These signs can take on different appearances, which became evident in a central piece of the exhibition in Marseille: *Puzzle, IMAGE NOT FOUND*. The thirteen letters of the exhibition title were executed in scale and presented on twelve pedestals and a flag pole. A number of these letters were also produced at their 'true size' turning them into 'monumental sculptures'. Language and image, signification and sign are all mixed up by Lieven De Boeck so they can be rearranged in a radically different fashion.

The exhibitions *Image Not Found* and *Objet Trouvé* had a strong emphasis on activating the artwork: by the very diverse presentations on the one hand and by the actions of Lieven De Boeck and Julia Reist on the other, in which the works were manipulated and 'used'. To Lieven De Boeck the artwork is not a piece of scenery but an object with a potential waiting to be activated. If the work is not activated, it remains stashed in a physical storage and/or the artist's mental archive with the inherent uncertainty if it will ever be able to 'exist'. An exhibition creates space for the artwork to function and because each space is different, each work and each spectator will function and respond differently. The image that we construct as we contemplate an artwork is far more intricate than the object itself, as it is being enriched with the imagination of both the artist and the viewer. Art demands our attention and it is the same attention we need to live our lives consciously. The invitation that was sent for the exhibition *Objet Trouvé* for example, consisted of an apparently empty envelope; only the attentive recipient would notice that the inside of the envelope was imprinted with the image of a blue sky with white clouds and a single bird. For most people, however, the image was lost. Lieven De Boeck's work is constantly situated in a state between appearing and disappearing, which also transpires in his preference for the rather 'immaterial' appearance of his work, in the form of light, glass, the white, the blue...

With his work and his exhibitions Lieven De Boeck is leaving mental traces that act as an antidote to utter oblivion. We are increasingly flooded by digital images that no longer relate to the analogue world and with their meaninglessness turn us into languid 'image consumers'. It may well be that today, we are all unwitting servants to the building of a new Tower of Babel, all speaking the single language of capitalism sustained by consumption. As a sign of resistance and liberty (and without Divine intervention) Lieven De Boeck has developed his own imagery and in doing so, he also created his personal realm of imagination that to us may seem confusing and at times even paradoxical but that, above all, bears witness to his freedom to generate personal meanings in order to counter the monotonous image consumption of today.

Opposite and next spread:
White Flags # 1, 2006
Onion skin paper, 192 cut outs
Dimensions variable

White Flags

A cloud of 193 white flags – the flags of the member states of the United Nations (as of August 2014) – with cutout forms are hung above visitors' heads. Every visitor can in this way "discover" the bleached out elements of his or her national identity, and wonder how the formal categorizing of the flags into abstracts shapes – bars, crosses, stars, crescents, suns, and other figures – creates a new or different reading of what it means to be global neighbors, what it means to belong to the arbitrary borders of a joint world order.

    The visitor can then begin to define what this denuded, colorless identity could mean nowadays. A white flag is of course a potent symbol with its own history as defined in the Geneva Convention, signifying surrender or a willingness to negotiate. So what does national identity really mean against the backdrop of recent events that have rocked our society and its norms and captured headlines around the world – the millions of refugees or the black flag of the Islamic States? Could the "General Assembly" of the flags likewise connote a religious experience through the sense of purity, unity, or oneness they convey?

Opposite and next spread:
White Flags #2, 2014
Tulle, nylon, and embroidery, 193 flags
Dimensions variable
Production in collaboration with Textiellab, Tilburg & Ester Goris

Top:
White Flags #2, 2014

Bottom:
The World Unmade # 05, 2015
43 Pantone colours painted on 43 basketballs
ø 21 cm

The World Unmade # 05 (detail), 2015

Next spread:
Untitled (Hand without Cigar), 2014
Silver silkscreen on black paper
49 × 39 cm (framed)

22 August.
22 August.
22 August.
22 August.

Van Wassenhove House.
Van Wassenhove House.
Van Wassenhove House.
Van Wassenhove House.

Sint-Martens-Latem.
Sint-Martens-Latem.
Sint-Martens-Latem.
Sint-Martens-Latem.

6:21 PM

28°

COPY/ORIGINAL

With me is the person I know, but there is also the artist LDB. That character plays an important part in the artistic work. Who is this LDB and to what extend are you, Lieven De Boeck – who claims to admit absolutely no autobiographical elements in the work – involved in this?

I might have put it that way once, but more recently I discovered that I am my own muse. By this I mean to say that my outlook on life is based on a number of questions, and these questions become part of my work as an artist. One important element is the idea of identity, of both the person and the artist. It is a concept that eludes me. I can't understand why I would have to feel Belgian or why I would have to be a man... I fail to see the point of all these compartments that society employs. To me, they restrict rather than to make things possible. What I try to do as an artist is to put forward the questions I have as a person and frame them in such a way that others can relate to them and reflect on them as well. This is one of the reasons why I call myself 'Copy of Original'. As an artist, I have declared my personal self to be a copy of the original.

When I met you in New York, years ago, I was briefly stuck behind your left arm. 'Copy of Original' it says, tattooed in the form of an old-fashioned stamp. So you are essentially the carrier of your own work. At the same time you reference several well-known cases in art history and the discussion about what is valuable/not valuable. The original, so the artwork itself, versus the copy is a theme that you visit quite regularly.

One of the things that define our identity is the way we compare ourselves to others. For an artist it means that you have the entire history of art to relate to. But the question takes us right back again to the issue of identity. You see, in my opinion there is no difference between the original and the copy. With everything that has ever been made, everyone should be able to carry on just fine.

Can anyone copy your work?

Of course.

You appropriate quite a lot. You, the copy, tattooed on your arm since 2011, during a stay in Los Angeles, make off with other people's originals. With 'Une Seconde d'Eternité (D'après une idée de Charles Baudelaire)' by Marcel Broodthaers, for instance. The initials M.B. have been replaced by LDB.

I don't write LDB, I Tipp-Ex out my initials. Because authorship is often confirmed by an autograph, I purposely erase the signature. The next question is why I base myself on Broodthaers rather than to make a copy of an Ensor painting.

Because you can't paint.

Even if I could paint. It doesn't inspire me technically, nor does it appeal to me intellectually. That's why I return to artists who addressed the same questions I do.

You could have mentioned 'Copy of Marcel' too. Because besides Broodthaers, Duchamp is another important reference.

I don't really like the name Marcel. (*laughs*)

You come from an architectural practice that you defined mostly on an artistic and theoretical level. Perhaps the transition to visual arts was very smooth?

I think I continued to do the same things I did in architecture at the time. This house of Juliaan Lampens, where we are right now, could serve as an example. Because this house hasn't been divided into cells. There is no programme to determine that this is the kitchen and over there is the bedroom. There is a sleeping area but it is open. Someone can be cooking here and someone else may be sleeping there, but they stay in touch. So I imagine this house as an empty space and because I define it as empty, I can make it my own.

LDB Signature, Une seconde d'éternité, 2009
16mm film, b&w, silent, 1"
Production by Atelier Graphoui and Sébastien Koeppel

THE RHYTHM OF MEASURE

What was your first autonomous artwork?

It is a piece that, though still very architectural, to me represents a key work. It is about the destruction of the Twin Towers. In those months after 9/11, I tried to understand, in my language, what had happened on that day. I found this attack, which I politically and morally reject, to be extraordinary powerful on a visual level. My work consists of the reconstruction, in floor plans and cross-cuts, of the towers' deconstruction. I have also visualised why the towers collapsed. The first one was hit in the steel core and the second one, that came down first, was hit in the perimeter wall. So the attack was directed against both structural elements of the buildings. One of the pilots, by the way, was an architect who had written a thesis about modernism's anti-Islamic programme. Despite the fact that modernism is mainly areligious. I also made a 1:200 scale model with Manhattan's grid on the floor and with the two towers. They are 2.2 metres tall, which puts you at the same height, as a viewer, with where the pilot was at the time. The project specifications consisted of a score that contained all the information about both the North and the South Tower.

Now that you mention modernism, we have to talk about Le Corbusier. You spent some time in Marseille, home to his Unité d'Habitation. In your work you speak critically of his version of modernism.

Le Corbusier gave architecture a social responsibility. He saw the world as a large space, with the countryside on the one hand and the city on the other. He also fostered a strong belief in the idea of collectivity. I found the same belief in the ideas of Luc Deleu, with whom I collaborated for a while. But Le Corbusier failed the moment he started to apply modernism as a style. I would like to refer to that intriguing book about modern emptiness by Camiel van Winkel. The reason that Chandigarh eventually became a success was because the Indian population adapted it to their own needs.

To base your entire thinking about architecture on the concept of the ideal human, a man of 1.83 metre, is rather scary. That's why you adapted Le Corbusier's Modulor.

I used it to reflect on the idea of universality. It connects again to that empty space we mentioned earlier. Such a space can be located anywhere and can be inhabited by anyone. But that same space will always be defined by a number of standards as well, like measurements. Take a kilometre: it is a universal concept but in terms of experience, everyone will describe it in a different way. This means I measure the empty space around me by my own standards. Because just like I don't understand identity, I have no appreciation of standards.

What are your measurements?

1.76 m. So I'm 7 cm short according to Le Corbusier's ideals.

Setting out from this house of Juliaan Lampens, where the light fills the void, I realise that the concept of absence is very important in your work. Some of your works just exist in a negative form, or in the delineation of the void. I also think of your styrofoam 'Letter A' that you 'borrowed' from Duchamp.

This preoccupation with absence relates directly to the fact that I believe there are too many images. And what's more, many images are being used to limit the creativity of the individual. These are images that dictate the way we should look or how we should behave. Even a box of toys prescribes, through its packaging, what you should do with its contents. It testifies to a lack of faith in the individuals' creative abilities to make their own images. The absence of creation, of authorship and identity in my work, that often consists of the air or its encapsulation, fits that way of thinking. Add to that the idea of the mould and of the repetition, inherent to the mould, which is explicitly made to produce series and copies. In this sense, the mould is more original than the work itself.

Which brings us to the *moule(s)* of Broodthaers. At the Frac in Marseille you showed both the Lego blocks that you had produced there in the glass factory, and the moulds they were cast from. The idea of presence and absence in one.

The Lego blocks included quite a number of elements. LEGO, which originally only produced wooden blocks, has long been subjected to lawsuits about copyright and authorship, things that interest me anyway. By now, you can imitate the blocks and only the logo is still protected. My first idea was to make blocks out of glass. That's why I made 3D-prints, in order to make a mould. But when I saw that plaster mould, I was so inspired that I also wanted to make them in glass. So 'Le moule en verre' came about very instinctively.

Letter A 1/1 (After Duchamp), 2016
Polystyrene, (4 ×) 45 × 45 × 150 cm

Moule en Verre (Transparent et Noir), 2016
Crystal glass
(2 ×) 9 × 9 × 9 cm closed
Production in collaboration with CIRVA
Collection Gensollen, La Fabrique, Marseille

You call it instinct, but your oeuvre seems to be the result of very well-considered decisions.

I suppose this observation is based on the fact that I provide a lot of explanation with my work. People often comment that my work is cryptic, that it can't be understood without explanation. Perhaps the fact that I always provide this explanation is a performative layer connected to the work. But in reality I do work very instinctively. 'Défense d'afficher', for example, is a neon work that came about because I had accidentally seen a similar poster hanging from a steel wire on a façade in Marseille.

At the same time it is a reflection on the redundancy of images and, provided that you install the work in an official art institution, an institutional statement as well. Your work testifies to a very critical mentality. At times it becomes political. In the past few years, your 'White Belgian Flag' has become more and more topical.

The first 'White Flag' dates from 2006. I was in New York at the time, for a residency at the ISCP. Bush Jr. was president and there was a lot of commotion about a breach of the Geneva Convention. But the Universal rights of man, which I of course personally endorse, are a Western concept that has not been accepted by everyone. Out of my interest in public space and how it is being defined, for instance by the nation state, one day I visited the building of the United Nations. The flags of all the member states, 193 by now, have been raised there in alphabetical order: form Afghanistan to Zimbabwe. But that apparently objective formation is less neutral than you might think. To begin with, it uses the English names of the states concerned. That in itself constitutes an interpretation. And then I wondered why, at some point, they would have opted for a linear order? The only way to reach neutrality is by placing all those flags in a circle. And why this emphasis on national identity when, as the UN, you would actually want to focus on what unites us rather than what distinguishes and thus divides us. It was there that I started to concentrate on the history of how those flags had come about. Through the symbols on a flag you can discover which groups once decided to form a state together. They often symbolise the making of a national identity. Now, it wasn't my intention to erase all those differences but it did raise some questions. In 2006, by the way, there were only two identical flags: those of Chad and Rumania. Only the shade of blue is slightly different. But once they are white, they are identical. In the Belgian flag, I retained the original shape of the three bands and I made sure the transparency was different for each of them, but the Tricolore turned white.

COMPORTMENT AND THE CARRIER

You work with neon, glass, paper, textile. If it isn't prone to shattering on the floor, it is likely to age quickly. With this choice of materials, you seem to announce a possible absence.

I do believe that our obsession with conservation, which developed in the 18th century, is quite absurd. It is a burden rather than a source of inspiration. Into each work, I try to build its disappearance – with my glass 'Mikado' as the height of fragility. The same counts for the slides, that decay in 20 years, and for the 16mm films – because I never work with digital media. Another example is the title of the exhibition in Marseille. 'Image not Found' is not a work to me, but a slide projection. The only thing that matters to me is for those words to appear.

Another feature of your work is its linguistic character.

I think this is a specific trait of Belgian art and the reason why there are so many good artists here. If there is anything connecting us, it's the fact that we all grew up with the continuous confrontation between the image and the word. A can of milk isn't just milk, it is also *lait*. If there is any such thing as a Belgian identity, it could well be this chronic confusion, the sense that an image never coincides with a word.

You play with words as well as with letters. In New York you created an alphabet, just like in Los Angeles, you made a rebus, and you wrote letters, one for each day of the year.

Several of my ideas about public space collided in that project. From the instant a second person is present, there is some kind of public space. The first person, however, will disguise themselves from this moment on, in order to create an image of themselves. I was wondering how I could translate this process into a written form. The letter provided me with a formal solution. In those 366 letters – in my mind it was a leap year – I did everything I could possibly do using language in public space: I can tell the truth, lie, seduce, contradict myself, reason in circles or be completely inaudible. These letters were never sent but I addressed them to myself. They always start with 'Dear Lieven' and they consist of found material, text fragments, interviews... None of it is original. I have published them in books. One for each season. And signed with Le Corbeau, which refers to Broodthaers but also to a French film (*by Henri-Georges Clouzot*, 1943, CP) that is situated in France during the

German occupation. Mysterious things happen in a village. A letter from an anonymous writer who signs with 'Le Corbeau' adds even more to the confusion. To me, this turned Le Corbeau into a symbol for the writer of the anonymous letter. And then I linked this to a letter I found on the internet, of someone who refused to take on any identity whatsoever. Subsequently, Le Corbeau can also be seen as a reference to Le Corbusier, the identity Charles-Édouard Jeanneret took on when he became an architect.

You also constantly play with your own identity. You appear in your work through the iris, the erased autograph, the flag… You also refer to Duchamp, the artist-chess player, with the work 'Le Perroquet/The Parrot' (2009) that consists of a chess board, the white squares of which can be 'read' as an artistic frame of reference. In homage to Duchamp you also made your own Boîte-en-valise.

I made several, actually, just like Duchamp did. They were all based on his first Boîte-en-valise though, which he made from cardboard and that I was allowed to research at the Getty Foundation in Los Angeles. I made my first one in wood. 'La boîte-en-valise en bois' sounded pretty to me. At the time, I was focussing on the way various artists approached the museum as an institution. I started out with the architecture and with the standard work of Ernst Neufert, one of the first Bauhaus students who later became Walter Gropius' assistant and writer of the book 'Architects Data'. When I was a student, this was still a standard work, that determined, for instance, how a house had to be drawn. In the original version the museum hadn't been included as a typology though. That was only added in a later update. In my own copy the museum was already mentioned briefly in the chapter 'amusement and recreation'. I thought that was quite remarkable. I was teaching in London at the time and a colleague showed me an Italian version of Neufert's book. There, the museum appeared between the lemmas 'cemetery' and 'church'. In that moment, language comes into play again. So I used Tipp-Ex to erase everything I deemed irrelevant. I only kept the terms that could demonstrate that a museum is not just an exhibition space but also a place where you do research. I combined this with 81 small plans of buildings from the 19th to the 20th century, from houses to churches, that I stripped of all functions in order to identify them as museum. By then, some of those buildings had become museums, by the way, which clearly showed the total irrelevance of the museum as typology.

Duchamp made his portable museum, Broodthaers his 'Musée d'Art Moderne, Département des Aigles'.

That is another theme I took up. The eagle is a very powerful image that can be adopted by various 'identities'. From 41 letter papers I cut out different eagles: one from the flag of Albania, from an aviation club, from a noble family... This became the work 'Musée d'Art Moderne, Archives des Aigles Disparus'. This inevitably took me back again to Duchamp and his portable museum, where he also plays with the copy and the original, the ready-made and the reproduction. To get a better understanding, I wanted to make that 'Boîte-en-valise' myself. I have later decomposed that first wooden version and rebuilt it in modelling materials. 'La Boîte-en-valise en plastique' is the last one. It holds all the works that refer to Belgium. I have no intention to make another one.

To you, to exhibit also entails an artistic gesture. The presentation is just as important as the work on display.

The exhibition is the work that is justified by the dialogue with the empty space and with other works. The works themselves engage each other in a mirrored dialogue. A discourse is being developed that doesn't end in the formulation of a final conclusion. That is the reason why I became so interested in the performative element as well. The exhibition in Marseille was definitely a step in the right direction. There, I could activate the works through mediators. In a traditional exhibition I run into a number of boundaries. So I look for other formats. For instance, I have considered making an open studio.

The sun has moved quite a bit.

This villa feels totally different now.

The light is beautiful.

Nothing is standard.

7:25 PM

27°

Défense d'afficher

"Défense d'afficher," more familiar to English-speakers as "Post No Bills," is a commonly ignored imperative found on building façades and construction sites throughout the Francophone world. Lieven De Boeck was inspired by the graffiti and visual noise of Marseille when creating his homonymous light sculpture, coyly appropriating this plea for civic tidiness while subverting its demands for graphic silence.

Collaborating with a commercial sign-maker for the piece, De Boeck developed a neon light whose gas would steadily deepen after forty-eight hours of illumination into the rich and famously static Yves Klein IKB bleu. Looped into cheery lettering based on his own handwriting, in this way quietly asserting himself as the artist, De Boeck's Défense d'afficher – instead of disappearing into Klein's imageless-ness – radiates out at us, unmissable from where it hangs. The work is thus distinctly Belgian in style, a Ceci n'est pas un questioning of materials, means, and message as well as a winking statement about art's ability to render them all absurd.

At the same time, the work is perpetually incomplete, and therefore ambiguous about its intentions: it will, tragically, never be switched on long enough in a gallery setting to reach its true blue. Consequently, De Boeck's discourse on originality (hand-crafted versus workshop-commissioned; found verbiage versus unique compositions) remains half-finished since it will never be aired in full. Défense d'afficher in this way – like all those affiches never posted – resists creating a totally "new" image, preferring to assemble a collage of references – the street, Klein, commerce, De Boeck himself – which can only allude to the piece's potential meaning. Our minds are left to flick on and off like a light switch, scanning the sign's words for a solution to an unsolvable puzzle.

Previous page and opposite:
Défense d'afficher, 2014
Neon, pigment, 70 × 100 cm

Défense d'afficher

Air de Bruxelles. Rue de l'Abbaye

For exactly one year, a white Belgian flag was hung from the façade of the gallery Meesen De Clercq in Brussels. As a result, the tone of the white color was complicated, changed into a variety of grays and browns, the material of the flag frayed and in some places partly destroyed, rendering the flag into a metric of sorts for the pollution of the air in Brussels and a measure of the sometimes invisible qualities of what the capital of Belgium and Europe might mean.

Air de Bruxelles. Rue de l'Abbaye, 2009
Nylon and particles
130 × 150 cm
Collection Nicolas Libert & Emmanuel Renoird

Air de Bruxelles. Rue de l'Abbaye (detail), 2011
Nylon and particles
147.8 × 172.8 cm (framed)

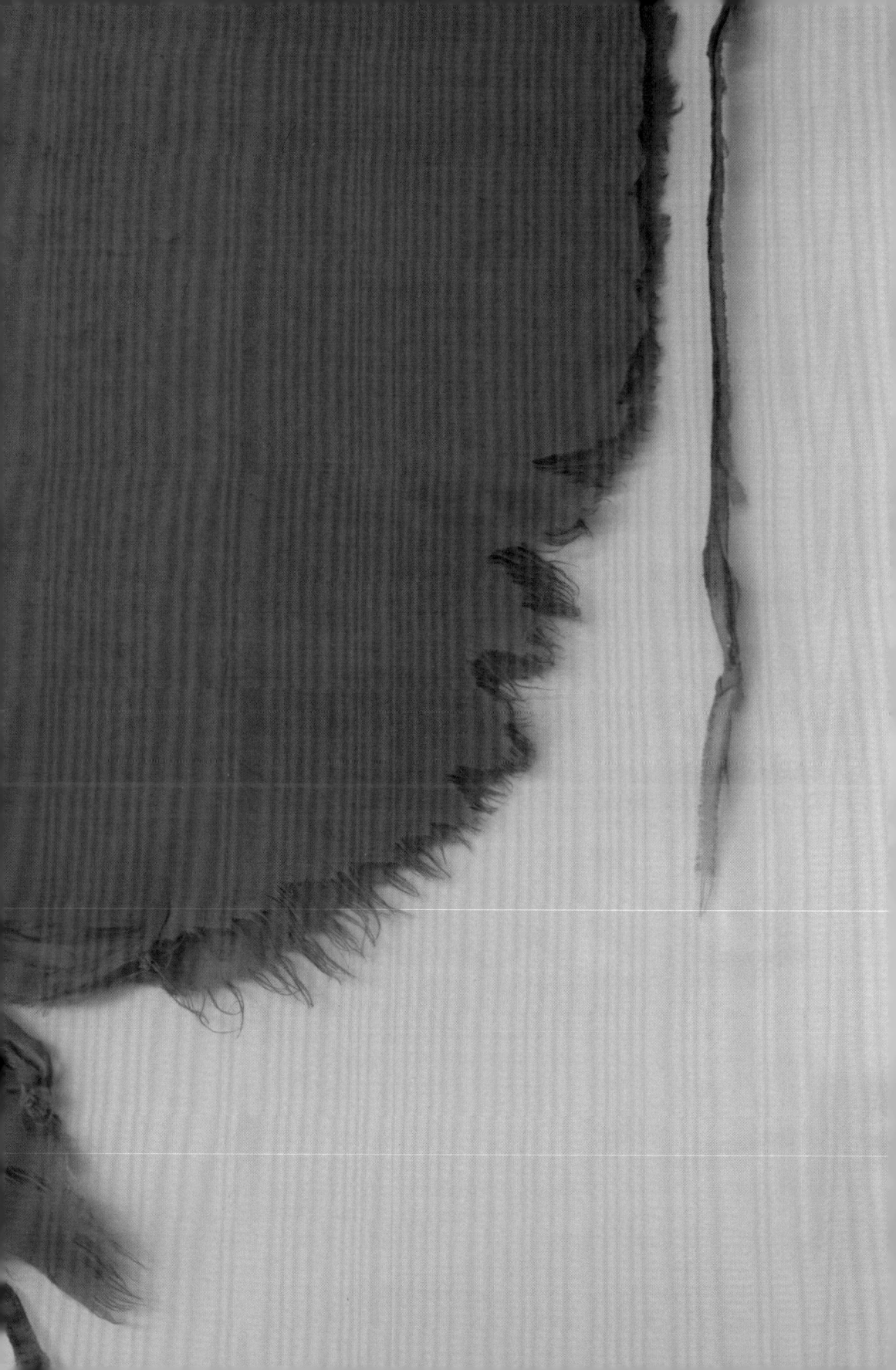

letusbeUS

The first neon sculpture produced by De Boeck came out of the artist's time living in New York in the first decade of the 21st century, during the second term of the George W. Bush executive regime. The neon plays with the double meaning of U.S. seen in "us." That is, the "US" is both the United States, global super power and a united "we," delivering on the philosophical promise of a nation born of immigrants.

The first sculpture was made in white neon, meaning when it is not switched on, it disappeared into the white of the gallery wall. When Barack Obama became president in 2008, the artist created second version in "black" neon. However, because black neon does not technically exist, the piece is in reality a version in white neon painted black by the artist on the front half of the letters. Consequently, when left off, the neon will remain visible, contrasting against the white gallery wall.

The meaningful contrast of white/white to black/white also provides a framework for revisiting the first iteration of *letusbeUS* (2006). This neon sign can be read as another portrait of the artist. Since it was made during his first American residency, the work is in many ways a personal reaction to aspects of the rise of post-9/11 American patriotism, but also a desire to become one with his environment, to find a way of entering into this nationalistic mood. The 'us' in this image is 'we' of course, but it is also the country in which De Boeck resided at that particular moment in time, as an alien, as an artist in a temporary residency without a green card. This is an image of a guest who invites his hosts to in turn become his guests. It may seem hostile to some – not in the least to American audiences – but it is intended as an act of hospitality, of surrender to the sensations of others, of a loving acceptance, of celebrating individuals coming together as a community as an act of real significance.

Top:
letusbeUS, 2007
Neon
47 × 17 × 5 cm

Bottom:
The Chinese Gloves, 2007
Two pairs of found gloves and broken car glass
Dimensions variable

The Blue_White_Red Story / France

"France" is a work made up of models of three poems: the story of *Bleu*, *Blanc*, *Rouge,* the colors of the tricolor flag of France. The white Styrofoam models are a physical representation of original poems as crosswords written by Laury Anderson. The letters of these poems, however, have been "translated" into the referential "letters" of De Boeck's own New York alphabet – a private reference to a published reference. Consequently, the panels lose their status as text and instead are read purely as quasi-legible images. Audiences find themselves in another country, a "France" confronted with an impenetrable other alphabet, devolving language into pictures – not unlike the experience of a person who cannot read barraged by the un-decoded symbols of ads and blinking signs all around them every day. From behind ladders hanging on the opposite wall, a voice whispers the stories one after the other, creating an auditory space that is a sonic mirror of the small transitional space of the montage room: an in-between room described in in-between terms.

The Blue_White_Red Story / France, 2016
Polystyrene, wood, sound
(14 ×) 81.20 × 92.20 cm

Next spread:
Hollywood Alphabet (A-Z), 2012
Cut outs of polyester tracing paper
26 sheets of 42.2 × 29.7 cm (each)
Collection FRAC PACA, Marseille
Collection Groeninge Group, Bruges

Hollywood Alphabet (A-Z) (detail), 2012

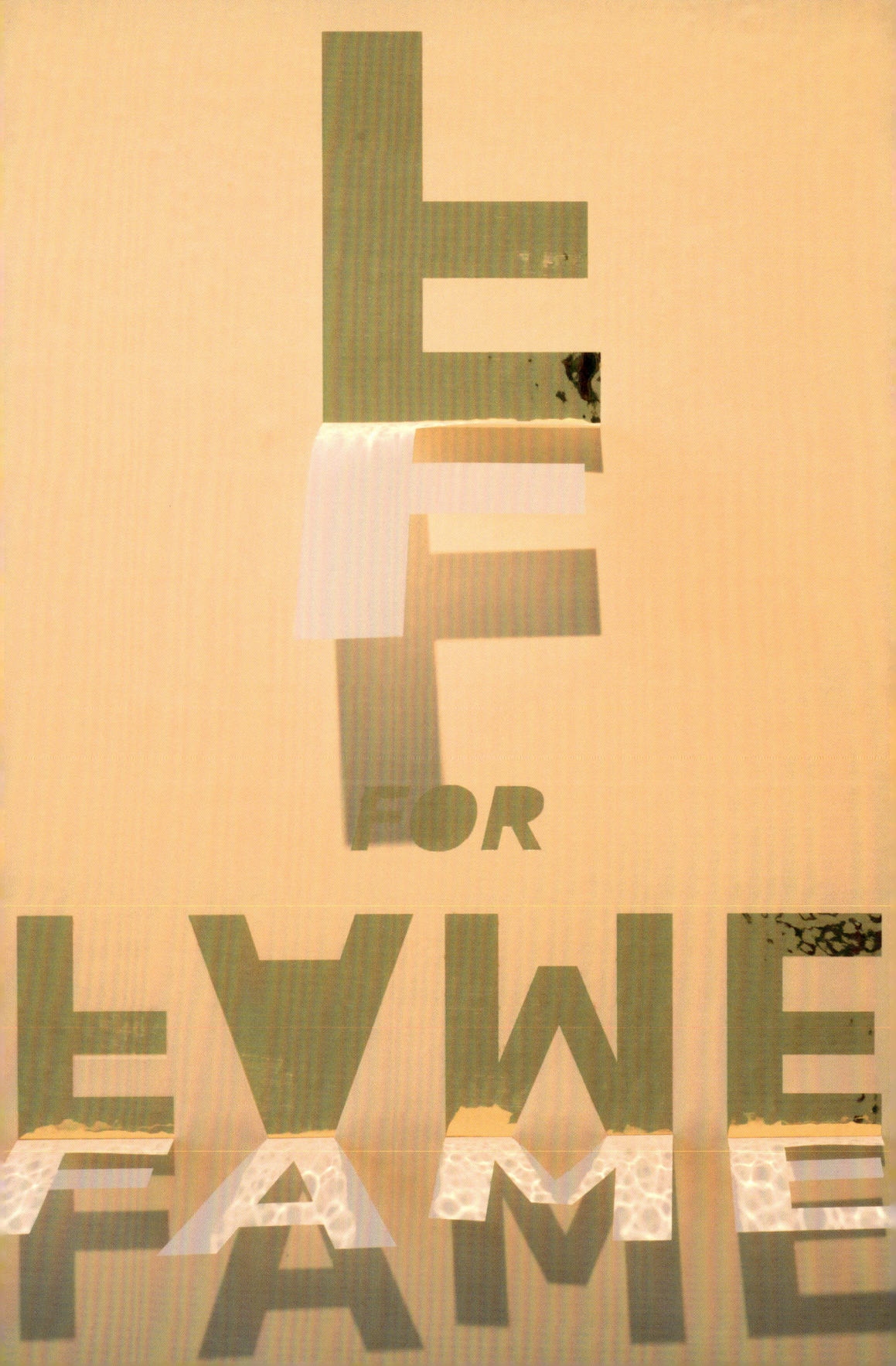

Jannah Loontjens & Jamal Mahjoub

The Original Copy of Mr X
The Original Copy of Mr X
The Original Copy of Mr X
The Original Copy of Mr X
The Original Copy of Mr X
The Original Copy of Mr X
The Original Copy of Mr X
The Original Copy of Mr X
The Original Copy of Mr X

As a child, he would stare at the sky and wonder. Was it really blue, or was that some kind of illusion? He experienced it as an intense emotion, rather than a colour. A statement, a challenge, a rebus for him to decipher in the fullness of time and space: why is the sky blue if the air around us is transparent?

Looking back, he sees his life as a sequence of questions to which he can only respond with approximations. It is as if his life has been dedicated to addressing issues that have no final answers; each one seems to lead him onwards towards the next station. Which raises the question; if his life adds up to a series of constructions, is there some way in which all of his works can ever mirror who he is? He grew up in a state of dislocation – belonging, yet not belonging. Born into a family and yet not a part of it. Where does a person begin? Is it determined by time, or place? The place where he was born, the hospital where his mother lay in labour, staring at the white ceiling, following the lines up one corridor and down another. How many times did she tell him the story of how he came into the world? The place was Dendermonde. Even the name of the town sounds like a puzzle: Den-der-Monde – an Underworld; an in-between world.

The people who have loved him, some of whom he has loved in return, they too add up to more than an itinerary of events, surely? Now, the early years of his life seem like a performance to him in many ways, a preparation for the life to come – like all childhoods, only different. His mother loved him: the quiet, pensive child, always wrapped up in his own thoughts. Both his parents were hard-working people, dutiful, following their own career paths, running on the treadmill – the kind of life he knew he could never have.

Was this where the sense of displacement began? The dominant presence in the first seven years of his life was Rachel. Each morning she came to pick him up and he stayed at her house down the road until it was evening and bedtime. In contrast to his own home, her house was full of life. There were cats, a dog called Teddy, a turtle named Jan and even a parrot called Coco, who would greet him every morning with the same question, 'Lieven, tu veux un Coca-Cola?'

In Rachel's house he discovered the freedom to do things. He would dress up in her daughter's old clothes and run about the house playing with the animals. He sometimes wondered what his parents would think if they could see this other him. He also wondered who he might have become if he didn't have Rachel in his life.

His parents mainly saw him during weekends. Sometimes he would be drawing in a book. They might be busy with one thing or another. When they came over to look at the drawing, one of them would say, 'I think it's already very beautiful,' and he would reply,

'I think I still have to add a house, or a tree or a flower...' Where did that conviction come from? He had no idea.

Nobody would disturb him while he was drawing. The whole household would wait for him to finish before they were allowed to leave, to go on an excursion, say, or do whatever was planned. So they all kept assuring him that the drawing was perfect, telling him it looked fabulous and that adding anything else might ruin it....

His mother often reminded him of how sweet and lovely he had been as a small child. She loved talking about her pregnancy and the delivery. If he had developed the idea that his mother's belly was his first home, then Rachel's house was his second. At Rachel's house he discovered that there were other places, places waiting to be discovered, places where he felt he truly belonged, where he could be himself. That ought to count for something. It was the first of a number of such stations of belonging. Like so many things, however, this was not to last.

Once, during the preparations for his show *Auto-portrait Contre Nature*, he suddenly felt the need to go back there, to visit Rachel. On the train heading towards Brussels, he looked at the clouds, the way they stay one and yet slowly transform themselves into something else. How often had he taken the train to Brussels, the train to London, the plane to New York or Los Angeles? In each city, he seemed to become another version of himself. He was transformed by the act of being in another place. So much so, that sometimes he didn't even need to travel. It felt as though the person he became in each city remained in those particular surroundings: Instead of one person traveling he had become several people, each living in a different city. He had become multiplied.

How to define himself? All he saw was a series of doorways, one framed inside the other. The possibilities of an empty doorway are endless, to some extent. On the other hand: they only exist within the parameters of their limitations, like an empty picture frame waiting for someone to fill it.

Where to begin? In order to track down a person you always need a place to start, a beginning, an end, some clue as to the direction in which the person is moving. Only, in this case it's not so much the places as pure energy which moves him along the trajectory of a personal faith. How many people wish they could have their own life story laid out before them, completely under their control? How many of us wish we could enhance the qualities we like, and erase the parts we don't? Don't we already do that? When we tell our story to somebody new we choose where to begin, where to end. We decide what is in and what is out. Life is a selective process.

Watching the sun going down over Manhattan, holding his phone in his hand. Across the East River the red orb sank between the rigid geometric order like a loose thought burning its way into a circuit board. Was this where it started? The point of departure, where architecture gave way to art, shrugging off its functional coat and becoming pure expression?

A wrong number. One of those weird coincidences. The kind of which novels are made.
– Is this Mr X?
He wasn't sure he had heard it right.
– Mr X?
– Is he there, the caller insisted.
Who was calling? Who did they want? Why his number?
The whole situation struck him as being more than mere coincidence. Mr X again. He could not shake off the idea that this was of some significance. But what exactly did it mean?
– There's nobody here by that name.
Even as he spoke, it occurred to him that there was a distinct possibility that he might have misheard. A name that sounded like Mr X. It could have been anything. The line was bad. He had had a few drinks. The caller was speaking English, but with an accent.
He hung up the phone. His friends were waiting for him.
– Who was it? someone asked, seeing the look on his face.
Wrong number, he said. He couldn't figure out how to explain.
– Happens all the time, someone else said. It was one of those things, forgotten by everyone in about five minutes. The talk moving on to who was wearing what and who was sleeping with whom. The minutiae of life. But his mind remained stuck there, in that question. Was it a message? Was the person on the other end of the line actually looking for him? Was he imagining that he again heard this name, Mr X? That mysterious name connected to one or two other moments in his life. Could it be possible that he was Mr X? He made his excuses, ran down into the street and started walking; uptown, downtown, no particular direction. He wished he could go back to the party, but he didn't know how to explain himself.

The voice on the other end of the line had sounded vaguely familiar, like listening to an echo from the other side of a wide canyon. The city had been good to him. It had given him a home, but more than that, it had given him contacts, a sense also of the horizon that stretched out before him. Inspiration.

While walking, he was aware of looking at the pavement. All those tiles, the concrete, the tar: the floor of public space. That's maybe what fascinated him most, what distinguished private from public space? Do we distinguish private from public in our designs? Or can any space become private? Not that he thought about those things when he began his studies.

During his studies as an architect he would realize that it wasn't about being original, it was about trying to connect to the real person inside; who he was, whatever combination made up his particular character, that was what he was trying to express. It wasn't until the second year that he found out how to express himself. Still, he couldn't really say who the actual person inside him was.

And then, after that phone call, it occurred to him that perhaps this might be the key to everything he had been trying to understand. He needed this other person, like a mirror, to see himself, to realize who and what his life was or had been. Perhaps he was Mr X and Mr X was the summation of everything he had been, of everything he would become; an abstract expression of his aspirations, his different selves.

Mister X wasn't particularly interested in fame, or success, although people often tried to convince him that his life was about to change; like with the first showing of *Auto-portrait Contre Nature* at the Luxe Gallery. They had great expectations. This could be the one, they told him, the show that passed him through the looking glass into that other world in which everyone understood what he was trying to say. But if that was the point, he thought to himself; I don't know what that is. And what I want to say has been said before; it's not specifically mine. It's the process of exploration that interests me.

The more people asked him about who he was, the less he knew. In interviews journalists would ask all kinds of personal questions, as if this was the key to who he was. What were you like as a child? At school? Were you happy? He would run away from such questions. When you hand the facts of your life to someone else for safekeeping you relinquish control. Another person decides what is and what is not important. They decide who you are and once they have defined you, who do you become? Who is the person in this account? Is it really you? Is there ever just one you?

Perhaps this was why he felt the need to go back, way back. Back to when it first occurred to him that he needed some kind of a track on his life. In school he had wanted to be someone else, prettier, funnier. He would have loved to be able to giggle like a girl... He loved to giggle! But he hated school. He knew he didn't belong there. Nobody there could see that he wasn't the person they thought him to be. They were trying to tie him down, to define him. But he knew. Even then, he knew he was somebody else, someone the others couldn't see. He did not want to be described as being as such and such, and so playing different personalities became part of the games he played every day. Adapting, transforming, making up memories became part of who he was. Both Rachel and his mother saw this as being creative, an indication of his lively imagination.

While walking through the streets of New York, thinking of Mr X as a summary of who he was, he remembered the day he took the train to see Rachel. It had been a similar feeling, then he had felt that he perhaps had to see her to realize where he came from, to understand the foundation of his life. The house across the road had looked much as he remembered it. The lights had been out except in one room on the second floor. He tried to imagine Rachel in there, and wondered what she might be doing. She would be an old lady by now and they'd had no contact for years, not since the age of seven when it was decided that she should no longer take care of him. Rachel's daughter had become jealous of the love her mother showed to the little boy. It had come as a real shock.

When he rang the bell, the door opened immediately. The light was bad, he couldn't make out the person standing in the hallway. It wasn't Rachel. Inside everything looked the same. Then he saw the parrot. The bird held its head at an angle and said, 'Lieven, tu veux un Coca-Cola?'

He wondered what the meaning of this might be. In light of the way his life had developed, spreading and multiplying, copying and reproducing, it struck him as significant that this parrot, the very symbol of imitation, this creature that characterised the qualities of a mimic, should be able to identify him instantly. In some strange way it was as if the parrot was the only one who really knew who he was.

The parrot and now the man who called him Mr. X.

And then there was the couple that he had once overheard talking in the train, years ago. They had been analysing a friend of theirs. It was an amusing conversation, their comments were smart and it appeared that while talking about the unknown friend they started to really understand him. They were seated right behind him. He couldn't turn around for fear of startling them. He sat perfectly still, filtering out the other sounds, the rattle of the wheels on the tracks, the whistle of the air against the carriage, the announcements over the PA system.

While listening to that conversation, it slowly dawned on him that they were talking about *him*. He didn't know the two persons, he did not recognise their voices, yet he was convinced it was about him.
– What year was Mr X born? Was it 1971 or 1977? one of them asked.
– Depending on which documents you refer to it could have been one or the other.
Had they really said Mr X? Or was his memory playing tricks on him?
– Remember the cartoons?
– What cartoons?
– The cartoons of Muhammed? He drew the cartoons and then covered them with Tippex, so the drawings became visible while remaining invisible.

He did that! It was him they were talking about! Or someone had copied him, which of course was a possibility as well.

They continued talking about his friend David. He had been the most handsome and popular guy in school and the fact that he wanted to be friends with Mr X was a big surprise to him, they said.

David was very sporty and was always the one who selected the members of his team. David decided that he wanted to make him more comfortable, he encouraged him to play football and to be more sociable. So, although he was quite useless at team sports, David always chose him as the first boy in his team. And so, somehow, very slowly, Mr X became someone else.

He had been fascinated and shocked. How could these two people know all those things about him? He stood up to get out at Brussels central station, and walked past the two people, but right at that moment they turned away from him, pointing at someone outside – look there is Olivier, one of them said – so all he could see of them was the distorted mirror image of their faces in the window.

And then there was that other moment when he had heard the very name Mr X before. Someone else had once called him by that name. At another station, this time in Berlin, at Tempelhof. He had been lost in his thoughts, walking towards his train, when a rather short man with a sympathetic face stepped in front of him. He started talking to him in French, clearly mistaking him for someone else.
– But aren't you Mr X? the man suddenly said in English.
– I'm not sure.

The man smiled. That does not surprise me, he said, turning away. Suddenly, he was curious to know.
– Why do you say that? Why doesn't it surprise you?
– You already know the answer to that, the man said, before disappearing into the crowd, leaving a simple plastic bag behind him, on the floor.

The bag contained a box of empty slide frames and a white card. On one side of the card was a name, Johnny, on the other side an address in London.

It was shortly after this had happened, that he began to examine why it was that people were so fixated on the idea of belonging. Why did they cling so fiercely to anything that could tie them down? He began to look for traces, studying the national flags of different nations, the signs that made people feel as if they belonged to one place or country, or culture, rather than another. What was it that made people feel as though they belonged somewhere?

Well, all of that was a long time ago. He did visit London several times, and even the address on the card, but he never found Johnny. He used the idea of the empty frame for his next show, which he entitled *Object Trouvé*.

All of this comes back to him while he paces the streets of New York. Mr X might have followed him wherever he went, he thinks, since he might just be a copy of himself. Or not just one, but many. He has been walking through the streets for so long, that night is shifting into day. He finds a coffee shop that is open and sits down near the window. He looks outside and watches the sky changing colour, from dark to light blue. He recalls the time he was in Los Angeles as an artist in residence at RAID. It was the LA sky that gave him his fascination for the colour blue. Air is so interesting, it's there and it isn't there, it's transparent yet blue. Air is like a mould; it's the absence that is the presence. In the mould, it is the air that does the work: it creates what is not there. Yes, that's what Mr X is. By being absent, he will always be present. He decides to sleep, he has to catch a plane that evening.

At 32,000 feet, leaving New York, heading back to Europe, he stares out of the window. A carpet of ruffled cloud extends off towards the horizon. The distant edge is tinted black by the setting sun, which remains just out of sight. At first he's not sure what he's looking at. Is it a cloud, or a range of mountains he has never seen before? It looks like a ridge of dark rock. He feels as if the whole world has just shifted sideways, slipping into another dimension. The clouds resemble the ends of the earth. Clouds look so solid, but are thin as air, they are one, yet many, and always in transformation. He realises that he is at peace with himself, silent and steady while in motion. For a moment he feels that he has become a cloud.

END

Moule en verre

The Work *"Moule en Verre"* is a glass composition comprised of six pieces. It was produced by casting each component in glass. The work functions like a three-dimensional puzzle, in which the individual pieces have their specific positions and only when arranged together do they manifest the formal, final object.
    The object was conceived during a residency at the CIRVA (*Centre International du Verre et Arts Plastiques*) in Marseille and is the product of research into the material of glass as well as into historic and aesthetic forms that pertain to age-old questions of beauty.
    The Moule en Verre itself is an "exact" replica of an actual mould that was used to cast another work produced during this same residency. By reproducing it in glass, the expected use of a mould was effectively *de-*functionalized and a new value was added, a value layered not only onto the new production, but also onto the original mould, since this mould would be the only model now able to make the "new" Moule en Verre.
    Among *dys-*functionalisation, extreme materiality, and rarefied aesthetic inquiry, the single gesture of recreating a copy in a new material, an interchangeable dialogue of fragility and beauty, emerged between the created "art work" and its original source. In this way, the Moule en Verre is not only unfolding and repositioning the question of beauty and fragility but actually embodying it through the lush corporeality, the touchably compelling physical character of hand-cast glass.
    By pushing the material possibilities of glass to its limits, this object becomes a kind of poem, a hymn to the vitality of questions whose answers do not come with words forming sentences, but through a constellation of elements that together elicit a thought, a feeling, evoke an ancient concept or reference an original inspiration.

Moule en verre (Rose), 2014
Crystal glass
9 × 9 × 9 cm closed
Production in collaboration with CIRVA

Next spread:
Moule en verre (Transparent et noir), 2016
Crystal glass
(2 ×) 9 × 9 × 9 cm closed
Production in collaboration with CIRVA
Collection Sohier-Degembe, Brussels

Explorations, 2016
Performance, video still

Explorations, 2016

Opposite and next spread:
Moule en verre (Rouge), 2016
Crystal glass
9 × 9 × 9 cm closed
Production in collaboration with CIRVA

Opposite and next spread:
Moule en verre (Jaune), 2016
Crystal glass
9 × 9 × 9 cm closed
Production in collaboration with CIRVA

Sã (100)

On a blue carpet, six volumes are constructed out of glass bricks in transparent, red, yellow, and black (a discursive reference to the patriotic color ways of Belgium and France). These brick forms are arranged into Fibonacci sequences in order to underscore the rules of beauty while remaining abstract and without being fully constructed into recognizable objects. At the end of the blue carpet, the mediators play with a series of red wax "Legos" in different sizes, manipulating them to form an impossible structure that defies the rules of beauty.

Sã (100), 2015
Mixed materials including colored Crystal glass
Dimensions variable
Production in collaboration with CIRVA
Collection CIRVA, Marseille

Sã (100), 2015

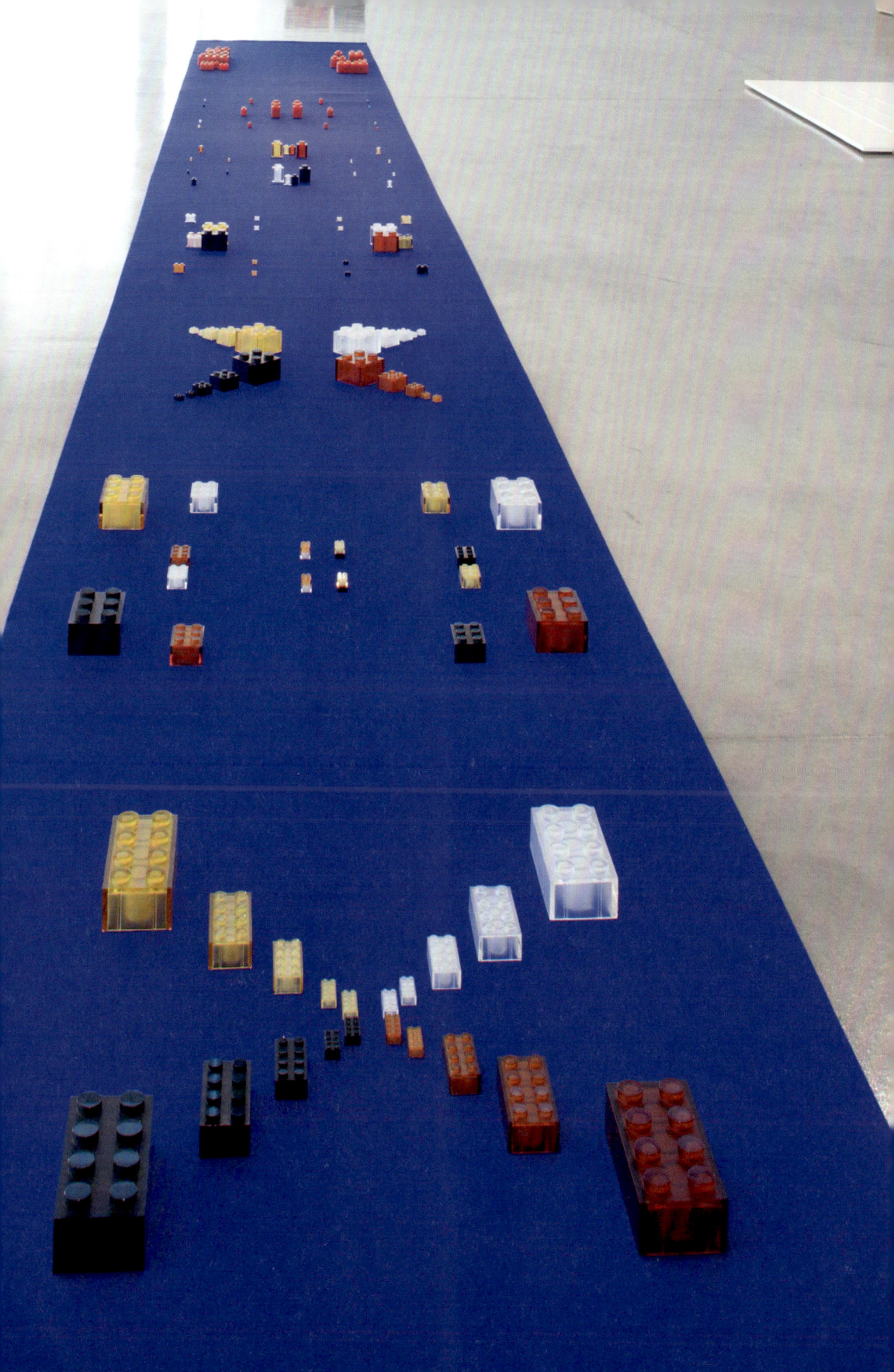

Opposite and next spread:
Sā (100) (detail), 2015

Sã (100) (detail), 2015

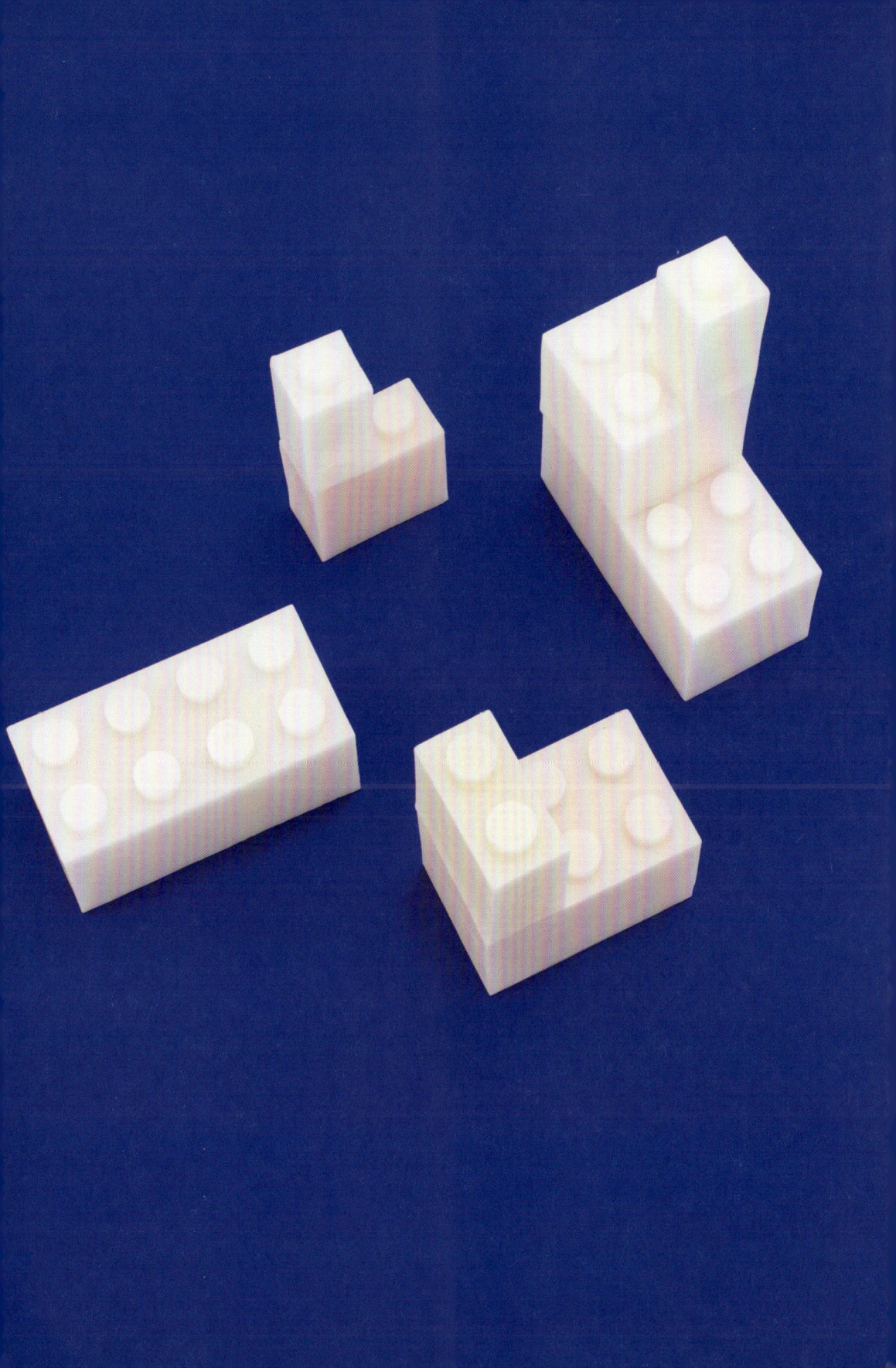

Explorations, 2016
Performance, video still

Explorations, 2016

Figure 1

The two figures are comprised of 10 identical transparent blown-glass sticks. They are positioned on two stands and showcase two divergent elements of classical beauty, one based on the purity of mathematics, in this case the Fibonacci sequence; and the second based on a harmonious composition, here the square.

The aim of displaying these figures is to underscore that they exist in a constant movement of placing and replacing, so that at every moment the figure and the series remain incomplete because of their manipulation by two people. At the same time, this movement creates a kind of dramatic tension due to the obvious fragility of the sticks themselves and the clear sound of thin glass striking a hard surface made when they are (re)positioned on the stands.

In its outward simplicity under constant threat of material destruction, the work also emphasizes the never-ending process of creation, and the ultimate impossibility of satisfying our desire to create enduring beauty through arbitrary rules.

Figure 1, 2015
Glass
200 × 200 cm installed / 4 × 150 cm, single Mikado

Figure 2, 2015
Glass
200 × 200 cm installed / 6 × 150 cm, single Mikado

Mikado LDB Modulor # 01

The Mikado LDB Modulor, is a sculpture comprised of 21 blown glass sticks, each 150 cm long and ribboned with a Fibonacci pattern of colored glass scaling 1-1-2-3-5-8. As they are extremely fragile and, despite their cheerful appearance, impossible to play with, they reflect the contradiction inherent in the famous Modulor of the architect Le Corbusier. That Modulor, a system of anthropomorphic measurements based on the dimensions of a man 183 cm tall, claims to be the source of an architecture adapted perfectly to the human body, despite the fact that 90% of people living are, in fact, not 183 cm tall. This older Modulor likewise includes the Fibonacci sequence and also tries to combine the metric with the Anglo-Saxon Imperial measurement scales into a single system (but of course it does not really succeed in merging these two together). As Lieven De Boeck's (LDB's) own foot is exactly 25 cm long, it assumes – within the logic of Le Corbusier – that taking the artist's foot as the standard "foot" would resolve all the inherent incompatibilities that arise when fusing a metric and an Anglo-Saxon system. The different sticks of the old Mikado children's game are thus scale bars based on De Boeck's own feet, with a corresponding "yard" and "inch", scaled to 1/1 and 2/1 and derived from this same set of "personal" standards. The joker of the game is a perfectly black stick, a nod to the absurdity of establishing a meaningful system of shared commonalities to begin with.

Mikado LDB Modulor # 01 (detail), 2013
Glass
Pied de stalle 200 × 200 cm / 150 cm single Mikado (28 sticks)
Production in collaboration with CIRVA
Series of 4
Collection Hervé Lebrun, Marseille

Mikado LDB Modulor # 04, 2013
Glass
Pied de stalle 200 × 200 cm / 150 cm single Mikado (28 sticks)
Production in collaboration with CIRVA
Series of 4
Collection CIRVA, Marseille

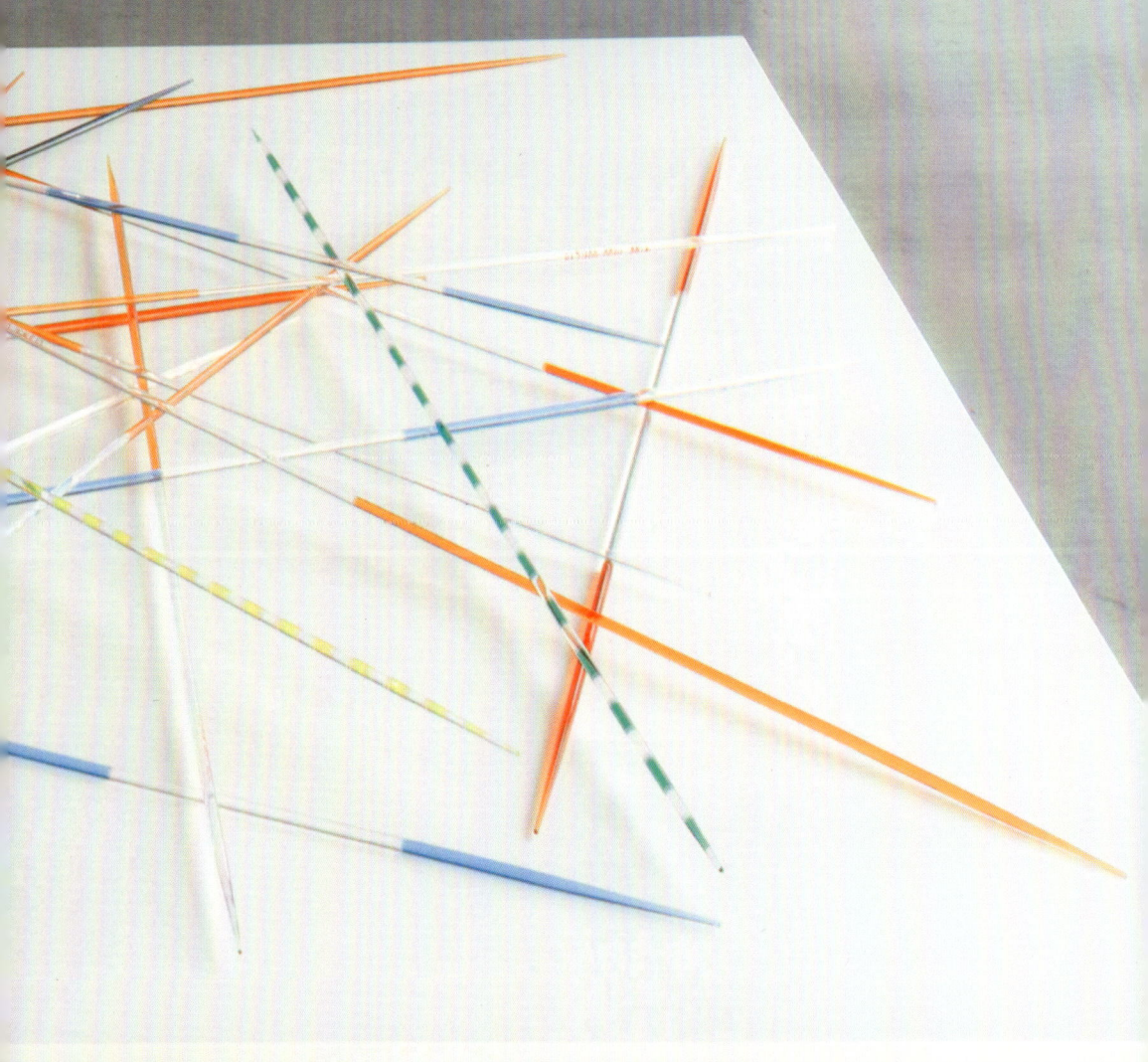

Meters

These works operate as scale bars in neon, measurements representing the artist's individualized "LDB meter" and referring to the chords of Duchamp's "meter," his "3 Standard Stoppages" created through a similarly arbitrary process based on personal actions. One neon knot looks like the infinity sign, suggesting the unending set of possibilities, while the other hangs on the wall, suggesting a kind of closed off loop of preset functions. Another one looks like a walking stick and the last two ones resemble springs. Together, these neon works are meant to work as a functioning system of measurement, and despite being images of a flexible or movable origin, they are all fixed moments of time and movement.

LDB Meter #6 / Knot 2, 2015
Neon
39 × 8 cm / 8 mm section

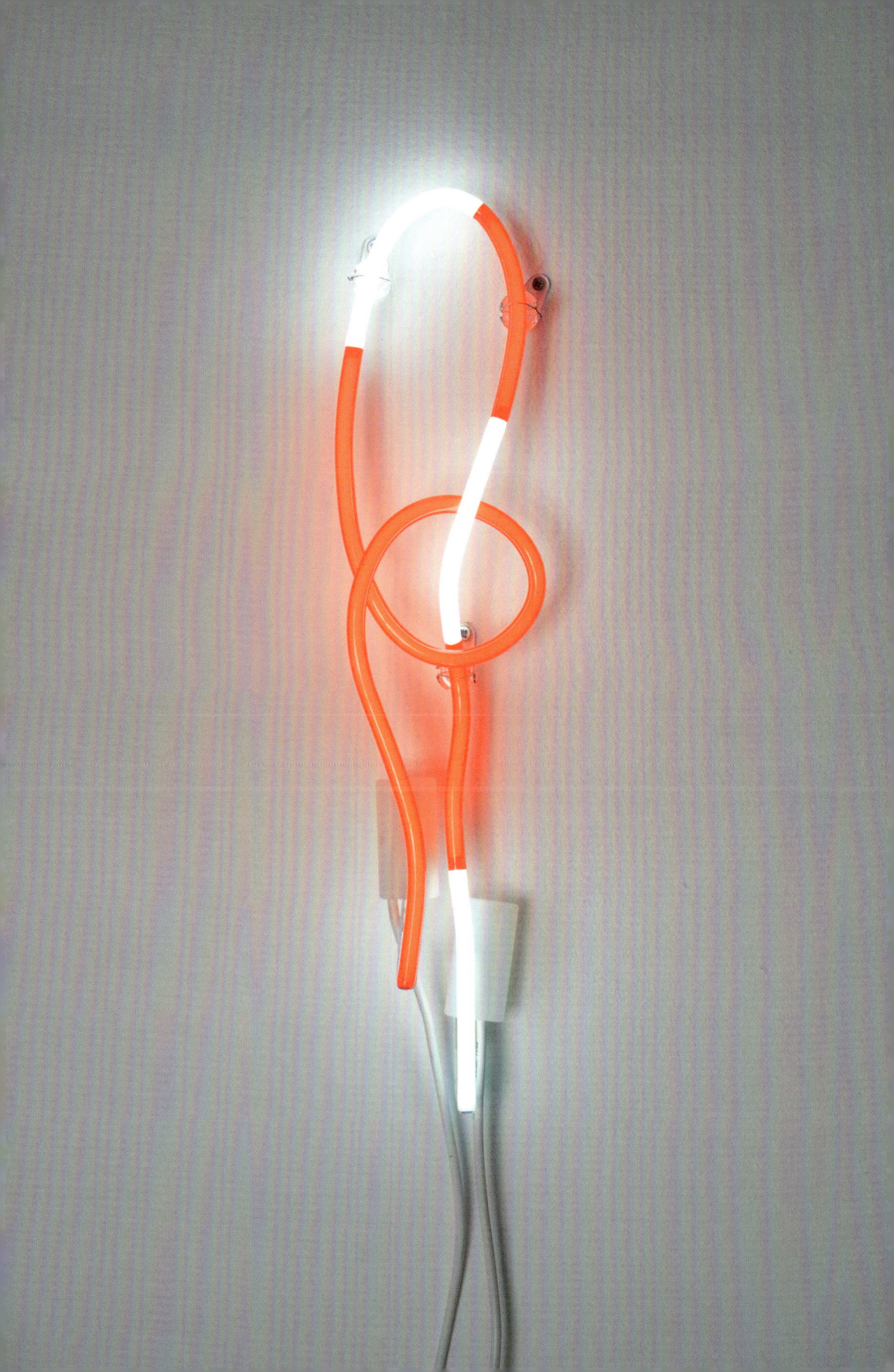

LDB Meter #5 / Knot 1, 2015
Neon
39 × 8 cm / 8 mm section

LDB 2 Meter #8 / Spring, 2016
Neon
15 × 11 × 22 cm / 8 mm section

LDB Meter #7 / Coil Spring, 2016
Neon
8 cm × 6 cm / 8 mm section

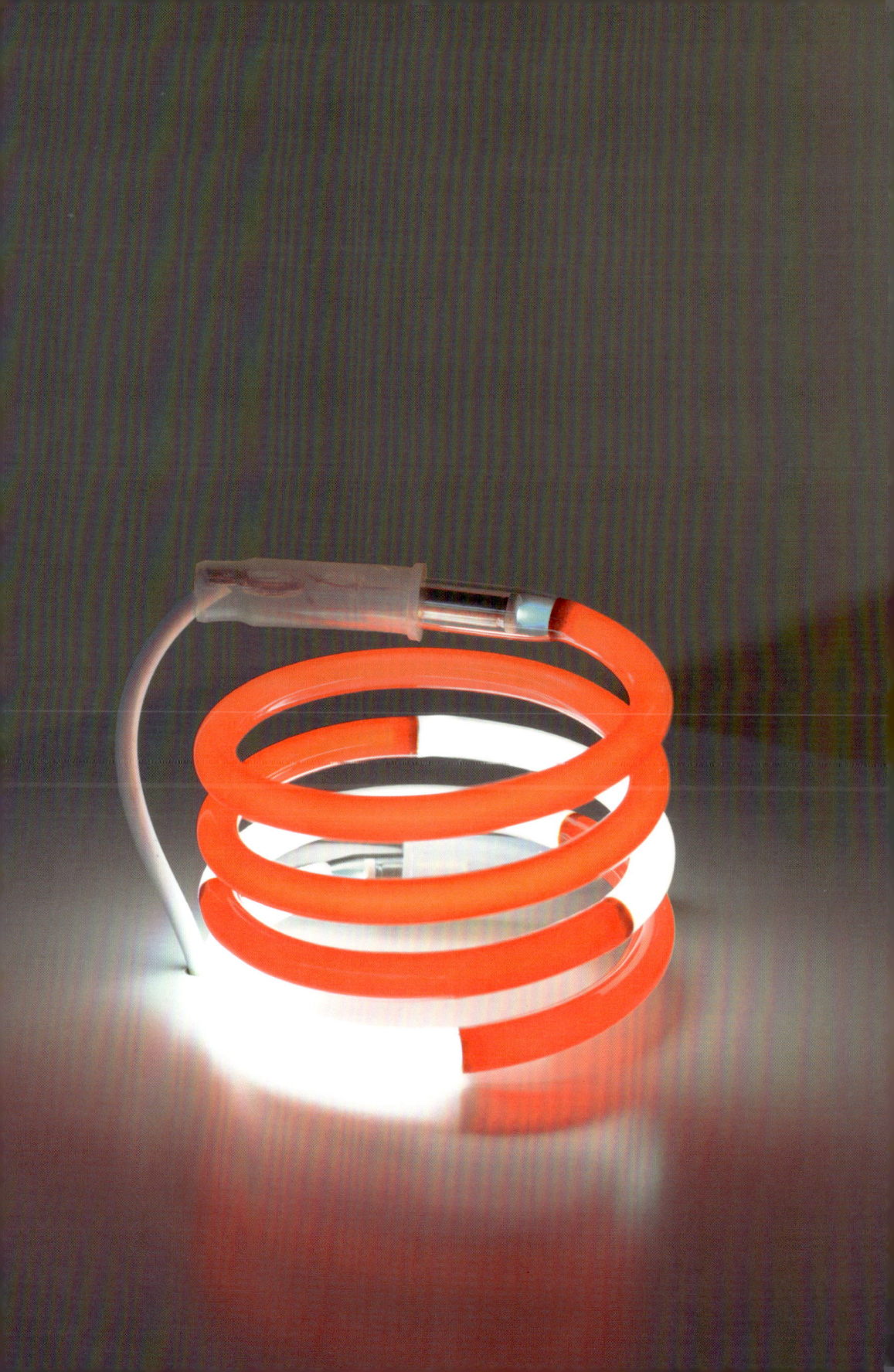

Mètre #2 (Canne), 2010
Neon
83 × 12 cm / 8 mm section

Enfin je vois clair en moi-même, j'ai peur d'être vu

"Enfin je vois clair, ..." is an installation that invites participation and contemplation while at the same time disrupting the ability of a mirror to provide a clean, clear reflection, to adequately provide the "self-regard" expected of an untroubled surface. The installation is produced from two movable mirror curtains and one fixed, semi-transparent mirror curtain designed to vibrate with air currents from the ventilation system. The curtained scene is entirely hidden except for hands holding the drapery aside. By repeating a text, a participant can manually slide the two curtains to the opposite side of the room, revealing the third, semi-transparent vibrating mirror to reflect back the whole room. The action in total creates a kind of waterfall effect in the micro-movements of the mirrors. The work is in this way a tool of confrontation with the audience: they are both performer and passive viewer, constantly shifting from one identity to the other, an agitated flexing reiterated in every shimmer of the fixed-yet-not-fixed mirror they have themselves actively unveiled.

Enfin je vois clair en moi-même, j'ai peur d'être vu, (detail), 2016
Mirrorfoil, thinmirror
2 × (550 × 130 cm), 1 × (600 × 152 cm)

Enfin je vois clair en moi-même, j'ai peur d'être vu, (detail), 2016

Pascal Neveux

The Revolution of Appearances[1]

Strictly speaking this is not a critical essay on the work of Lieven De Boeck, but rather a series of impressions, at once precise and indefinite, of an amicable intellectual relationship that has firmed up in recent years, and more particularly since his first solo exhibition in France, "Image Not Found", at the Frac Provence-Alpes-Côte d'Azur[2] in Marseille in the spring of 2016.

To offer De Boeck's artistic agenda to the eye and the mind in a single publication is to bring into sharp focus his fidelity to the personal grammar underlying the pronounced inner consistency of his work, from the initial projects through to the numerous exhibitions and residencies now fuelling his career.

This deep thematic unity has its roots in a singular conceptual world which the oeuvre deploys via a no less specific iconography. However, thematic consistency and repeated use of the same tools have not resulted in repetition of a formula or resort to a given generic territory. On the contrary, the striking thing about De Boeck is his extraordinary stylistic variety, as if the completion of each work entailed coming up with entirely new formal devices for facing fresh challenges and revealing new levels of interpretation. Following the development of this artistic approach chronologically allows us to assess his astonishing allegiance to areas of experimentation which borrow their semantics and tools from the worlds of the social sciences, architecture, and politics in the etymological sense.

Whether involving objects often addressed in series, or videos, sculptures and installations, De Boeck's output apprehends the real in its most immediate form through the image. So it is very much a question here of a representation of the world. Indeed, his works interrogate the value we have for so long, and naturally, attributed to works of art as an index of the real: their capacity for veracity or verisimilitude. The De Boeck oeuvre allows us to summon up a representation of the real in a different way, by bringing forth other potential images – other images of images. These latter thus stand revealed as an interface for the reconciling of the real and the imaginary, the two poles Edgar Morin situates at the origin of all representation: "The image is not only the nexus between the real and the imaginary. [...] The real emerges into reality only when it is interwoven with the imaginary, which solidifies it, gives it consistency and thickness – in other words reifies it."[3]

De Boeck's renewal of the procedures for summoning up our representations of the world re-embodies the images in question and so makes possible a renewal of the experience. His artistic explorations offer a close fit with one of the few acceptable definitions of Art: a way of ideating the world, all disciplines included; a thought mode fuelled from the outset by a personal lexicon made up of families of objects and images

1. André Breton, third issue of the magazine *XXème siècle*, 1952.
2. FRAC: Regional Contemporary Art Collection.
3. Edgar Morin, *The Cinema, or the Imaginary Man*, trans. Lorraine Mortimer (Minneapolis: University of Minnesota Press, 2005), p. 227. Original translation slightly modified.

that call for a reconsideration of the formal language of an artwork in the light of its symbolic system, its perceptions and its tension between sign and language. De Boeck's work also takes words as its raw material in graphic as well as semantic terms, exploring the interstices between them, between their letters, between the word and its translation, between the word and the space containing it, between word and image.

This is done in installations which take issue equally with the exhibition venue and the exhibition itself. They transform the exhibition space into a research laboratory, using procedures inspired by scientific and academic systems and cultivating a type of presentation similar to that of the archive – but a living archive, at once personal and universal, to be reactivated according to the exhibition contexts concerned.

In concrete terms his exhibitions propose choreographies of objects, systems and itineraries whose principal function is to set his thinking to work via the medium of the site. Every exhibition is shaped by a work in progress that takes account equally of the site's specific givens and the reactivation of earlier works. It should perhaps be mentioned here that his works possess the rare quality of autonomous existence and, seemingly without end or purpose, can be invested each time with fresh meaning according to the presentation context. Thus the exhibition is firstly the appropriation of a place in its concrete physicality and its geographical, historical and even symbolic reality. De Boeck designs his interventions as narratives which can never be completely grasped, but which set out to foreground and dissect modes of perception while seeking to involve the viewer in an experience combining the physical and the conceptual. "There is no thinking without form," claims artist Jean-Luc Moulène, a statement De Boeck could readily espouse, given that he accords as much importance to the research and production phases as he does to the designing of his exhibitions. He is characterised by an imperious need to take the time to fabricate and test new materials and new media, while surrounding himself with craftsmen and technicians who accompany him into the unknown terrain whose boundaries he loves to push back further and further. His encounter with glass in recent years, in the course of several residencies at the International Glass and Visual Arts Research Centre (CIRVA) in Marseille, has resulted in a family of objects whose intrinsic virtues testify to the maturity of his artistic approach.

In his body of work as a whole, De Boeck is out to capture the connection between image and politics, signifier and signified, with set theory serving as a protocol for putting the works into circulation and generating interaction with them.

His *White Flag* installation, comprising 193 United Nations flags, and the neon piece *Défense d'afficher* (Post No Bills) of 2014, are a clear indication of his aesthetic and political dimension reach. They possess that inner force that transcends their status as artworks and turns them into thoroughgoing, artistically irreproachable manifestoes.

Thus the "Image Not Found" exhibition in Marseille prompted interaction between a corpus of pieces produced over the last ten years and shared spaces that organised visitor movement within a highly elaborate formal and narrative arrangement. Bringing all these works together also drew attention to the remarkable diversity of his output and the way it develops. Whether in Marseille (2016), Montreal (2015) or Deurle in Belgium (2016–2017), each exhibition is an opportunity for him to play a different score, investigating his oeuvre in relation to the spectator and the institution in relation to the works. "Image Not Found" and "Objet trouvé" (Found Object) are in fact not two separate exhibitions, but rather a single project whose governing interpretative dialectic functions in two different areas of the same thematic corpus. In linguistics an interpretation is the conferring of new meaning on a sign, action or word – a link to the realm of semantics that would not displease Lieven De Boeck.

And so his works really do shape an exhibition space, one that they inhabit visually while avoiding the pitfall of excessive dramatisation.

If we begin with the postulate that art is a complicated business, then the De Boeck oeuvre is clear proof of the fact. And if art is a simple business, his oeuvre provides an elusive demonstration. So, clear proof that art offers spontaneous aesthetic pleasure for a public apprised or not of the mysteries of the works' creation; or elusiveness because even the "novice" detecting a flagrant disparity between their sophisticated beauty and such often elliptical titles as *LDB Meter/5/KNOT 1 and Lettre A 1/1 (After Duchamp)*, can conclude that something is escaping him behind these contradictory appearances. The "expert", though, has the advantage over the novice in that he has gained through experience the conviction that a work of art always resists even the most scholarly attempts at elucidation. This sensation of "resistance" is the rare quality to be found here in works free of all superficiality and illustrational character.

For De Boeck the presence of letters projected, drawn, sculpted or hidden is part of an especially meticulous interpretative strategy. Words intersect, respond to and echo each other, evolve in space in a replay of the Latin etymology of the word text: to write is to encode, to read is to decode.

Floorplan opposite:

Level 1
01. White Flags
02. Letter E
03. Letter N
04. Letter O
05. Puzzle Image Not Found
06. Letter T
07. Letter A
08. Auto-portrait contre nature
09. Letter I
10. Une seconde d'eternitée, Re-enacted
11. Série Bleue
12. Défense d'afficher
13. Cinq
14. Letter N
15. Moule en verre (bleu)
16. I Lie
17. The Blue-White-Red Story, France

Level 2
18. Enfin Je Vois Clair En moi-même, j'ai peur d'être vu.
19. Lettre anonyme
20. Mikado LDB Modulor
21. Sã(100)
22. Ldb Meter #6
23. Hollywood Alphabet (A-Z)
24. Moule en verre
25. LDB Meter #5
26. Figure 1
27. Figure 2

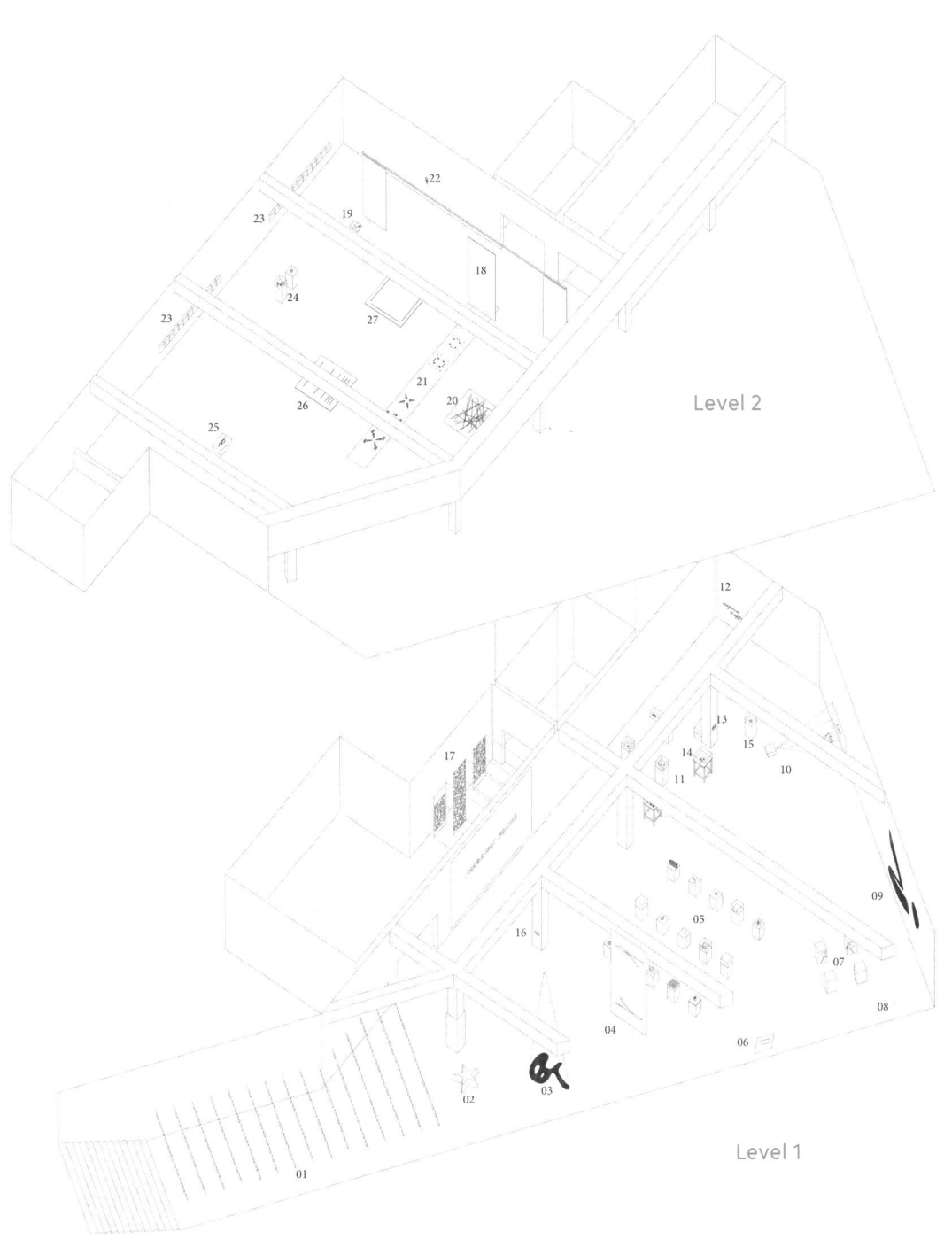

Axonometry exhibition lay-out, *Image Not Found*, 2016
Frac Provence-Alpes-Côte d'Azur

Jean-Luc Nancy has made the same observation in a short essay on the relationships between texts and images: "Text is the stuff of meaning." As it happens, Nancy's comments on the different nature of text in theatre and cinema are not without correlations in De Boeck's artistic project. In the theatre the body becomes text; it is the messenger, the imprint of a writing "made for [theatre], a writing formed by gesture, posture and breathing."

Through language as an object and subject De Boeck looks into the matter of transmission and reception of an event, of the experience of an exhibition, of a performance – what is transmitted, and how? What is the spectator's place, and what do we expect of him or her in return?

Private sphere, public sphere, Art History, language, alphabet, image, cinema, identity: these are the themes permeating works whose creator evinces the same interest in the process as in the final result. Characterised by open-ended thinking about the status of the artwork, De Boeck challenges the representation and the critical reception of his output through gestures and interventions making play with displacements, tweakings and appropriations. His work is an affirmation of a kinship with the Belgian and French avant-gardes and the American Conceptualists of the 1960s, a kinship receptive to a production rationale that transcends mere appropriation; a system of signs being constructed over time, one that generates an indirect commentary on the oeuvre and deterritorialises practice so as to enter different artistic, political and scientific fields. An approach that questions our relationship with the world and today's society and thus is part of an international art scene which from Pierre Bismuth to Joëlle Tuerlinckx, and including Philippe Parreno, Ryan Gander and Michel François, propose narrative gambits viewers cannot fail to react to, while urging them to assemble their own, independent critical and political baggage.

Also perceptible in De Boeck's work is the importance of the movement and placing of the viewer's body within the work itself.

We are not simply seeing a work; we are testing out a space, becoming the main actor in a system, in a performance whose genesis is known only to the artist.

The design of his exhibition in Marseille, and more especially the decision to modify the classical exhibition codes – by changing the habitual direction of the viewing itinerary and allocating one of the two spaces exclusively to "a performance every day – except Mondays" – offered an insight into the way an exhibition can be a living form, a medium in its own right, a shared territory for writing, research and experimentation. In this case an exhibition whose suggested "performative" character might be indissociable from the discourse that triggers and determines it, with the artist leaving viewers to choose and define their own itineraries within his exhibition/system.

Indeed, an exhibition is always a narrative system whose meaning and deep preoccupations it is up to us to decipher. By adopting the postulate that inherent in all artistic creation are the principles of a form of writing, De Boeck expands his field of possibilities, demonstrating the porosity between disciplines as varied as dance, performance, poetry, architecture and the visual arts in general. In his exhibitions the sound dimension and its corollary, silence, are a given worth lingering over, one that foregrounds an original type of sound poetry to be found in pieces like *Lettre anonyme* (Anonymous Letter); more classically in *The Blue-White-Red Story, France* (2015); and even more notably in the activation of Space 2 at the Marseille show, which, in line with a protocol set down by the artist, orchestrated the strollings of mediators/interpreters, involved the handling of certain works, and led to the enunciation of brief sentences conceived of as veritable haikus.

In today's societies making noise, colonising space with sound and speaking more loudly are very often considered the mark of an action's success and value. If the presence of sound does not necessarily exclude that of content and meaning, and can even be one of their components, the effect – if not, indeed, the function – of sound is often to scramble perception and prevent thought. This is the exact opposite of what is going on in De Boeck's case, where where no sound interferes with our reading of the works; on the contrary, they are displayed in a silent space where the viewer concentration is enhanced by meticulous mise en scène and finely tuned handling of light. The silence is above all that of the artist himself, and this, whatever the circumstances, renders us open-minded and receptive. In linking us to ourselves, silence fosters real interchange with others and with the outside. This experience of the private within an exhibition makes its own demands: it is not something modish and has nothing to do with the canons of relational aesthetics; rather it is driven by curiosity, mobility and permanent questioning. De Boeck's approach is responsive to all territories of creativity and ideas. The artists, architects, art critics and curators he has had dealings with have encouraged him to broaden his awareness of the world and see his practice as a new contemporary humanism. As Jean-Marie Straub advises, "You first have to see, then look, then get to know. Then see again." Lieven De Boeck's work gives us a grasp of the viewing experience.

For an understanding of what De Boeck is telling us via the silence of his exhibition, speech is important. It is when words proliferate and voices resound that the substance of silence stands self-revealed. As soon as we begin paying attention to what unsettles us and what surrounds us, silence becomes the watchword. It is in this "ephemeral suspension" of permanent hubbub that the exhibition finds renewed vibrancy and the body's energy is recharged. Michel Foucault explains that in ancient times the masters of the Academy imposed three years of silence on their pupils, with no questions allowed: only the word of the master was to be heard. De Boeck's exhibitions are at once a lesson about silence and a lesson conducted in silence: we listen to somebody, in this case the artist, and in doing so reconnect with his concerns and his focus on the broader issue of transmission. Silence remains a highly political question, in the sense that it has to do with the organisation of our social structure. So before attempting to grasp why making silence seems a difficult business, we must evaluate its degree of necessity by breaking free of the many systems and installations that endlessly associate random sounds. Silence also raises issues and challenges in the realm of architecture. Traditionally architecture is the first among the arts, the one in which language has not yet found a place. Considered in the light not only of religious architecture – with its link between silent reading, silent prayer and churches – but also of secular places where silence reigns (libraries, hospitals, etc.), silence appears as a necessary preamble to all transmission. "Speak if you have words stronger than silence," says Euripides, "otherwise keep silent." With De Boeck the exhibition experience is part of this dialectic and is, simultaneously, a call to keep silent and to listen to words and sentences that are going to orchestrate the itinerary of a viewer who must confront his own solitude and come to terms with himself. The most important thing is drawing on the coexistence of silence and the possibility of a movement in space-time. Activation of the Marseille exhibition was the outcome of a conversation between the mediators interspersed with long silences. A mediator who was speaking would suddenly hold his breath for several seconds, then speech would inhabit the space again, conjuring up such-and-such a work. De Boeck has learned to gauge the active role of silence in the process of his activations. For the experience to be successful the viewer has to be kept in suspense and brought into the silence game so as to ensure a silent sharing that goes to the heart of things both gesturally and verbally. The appropriate cast of mind and physical state are enhanced by the wearing of gloves "customised" by the artist: a non-conceptual but radically experimental form of minimalism that can affect each viewer's intellectual functioning. A paroxysmal situation in which the viewer is also a witness to the exchanges in which he is participating only through his silent presence. A way of granting auditory receptiveness value as learning and transmission, of giving words their rightful place and thus valorising them in terms of their meaning and intrinsic beauty.

To what do these silences summon us? What is their function in the construction of a narrative or the evocation of the world?

A presence of silence, not as the absence of something, or a lack, but as augmented presence in the world around us. Seen thus, silence is not a stoppage, or stasis, or the end of something already manifested, but a dynamic, a prelude to the action to come. Something that suspends attention, sharpens the senses, fuels the sensory. De Boeck invites viewers to be "in" silence, to immerse themselves in sensation prior to ideation, to leave room for what cannot be formulated or quantified, for a kind of bodily state existing in the silence of a new, free, open-ended roaming amidst the works.

In De Boeck's case silence possesses the rare quality of being a moment of withholding, a new unit of measurement that preserves us from the immediate response, the urgency and the speaking too soon that can sometimes betray not profound commitment but a mere skin-deep reaction. Preferring permanent questioning and constant investigation, De Boeck appeals to our inner sensitivity as a means of rendering us more receptive to the words, images and objects that make up the score of his exhibitions. His agenda is not radical affirmation, but an intellectual continuity that leads him to question anew the real status of his works and their adaptability to different contexts, spaces and audiences.

Only a handful of authors and directors have given such close thought to these matters as that virtuoso Samuel Beckett, whose mastery of quantity and quality are so evident in the plays *Silences* and *Act without Words*, written in 1957. And Paul Claudel who, in a dictum as brief as it was to the point, liked to say that it was in silence that we could best be heard.

The question that quickly arises is that of the adaptation – or "free adaptation", as applied to literary works in movies and the theatre – of De Boeck's works and systems when they become a matrix, a meeting point or even a playground for curators, museum directors and the artist.

The spatial disposition of De Boeck's works is, for him, the expression of an invitation – or rather an injunction – to movement. Something simultaneously entailing roaming, the promenade and the *dérive*, or drift, once integral to Situationist theory and practice.

At work here is a copresence of places, planes and directions in space, together with the signs and markers embedded in them. More than mere univocal, authoritarian points of view forced on visitors, these signs and symbols are laid open to the eye, offering the possibility of relating to them and finding one's bearings.

De Boeck's creations are first and foremost an invitation to the discovery of a conceptual territory, a fertile lexical atlas at once concrete and fictional, personal and universal. Neither filmic nor strictly speaking theatrical, his approach is much closer to poetry and literature in the sense that these two art forms emphasise inner resonance and meaningfulness ahead of representation and spectacle, and atmosphere ahead of narrative.

The exhibitions "Image Not Found" in Marseille and "Objet trouvé" in Deurle are opportunities for an overview of the De Boeck modus operandi; not in the form of some detailed retrospective chronology or formal inventory but, on the contrary, as a means of challenging the actual status of the exhibition and the host institution. What is involved is not a retrospective but a free, clearly demonstrative interpretation bent on denouncing the illusions of painting and sculpture and the conventions of language: images delude us and words exploit our credulity. The ordering of the works is not chronological but logical, pointing up a consistent line of thought and ongoing creative obsessions.

To his credit the numerous works produced at CIRVA in Marseille in 2013–2015 – among them *Mikado LDB Modulor*, *Série bleue* (Blue Series) and *Moule en verre* (Glass Mould) – as well as the acquisition of *The Hollywood Alphabet (A-Z)* by the Provence-Alpes-Côte d'Azur FRAC in 2013, De Boeck devises his exhibitions as manifestoes. His intention is to challenge the museum space and its codified functioning, and to interrogate, as he does in *M.U.S.E.U.M.*, the status of the artwork and its formal, stylistic and conceptual typologies. His unhampered handling of concepts and the *mise en abyme* of these typologies enables him to take the visitor on a walking tour designed as a sequence of investigations at once poetic and political. What emerges are the notions of identity and language, and combinatorial games drawing on aesthetic, mathematical and political concepts. The golden section, the classical canons of beauty, the concepts of the original, the copy and the readymade, mathematical sequences (Fibonacci numbers), units of measurement, and architectural typologies (Neufert, the Modulor) – these are all areas of research invested by the artist in installations and objects endowed with considerable aesthetic and conceptual added value. For him the status of the object is fundamental;

and he causes this status to evolve in a combinatory dimension of sculpture-objects and concept-objects that can be activated in the context of performances.

Working via subtraction, sampling and cut-outs of shapes and colours – as in The *White Flag* (2015), with the 193 flags of the United Nations classified according to formal affinities after elimination of their colours – De Boeck calls the established codes and usages into question, the better to analyse them and to suggest highly personal modes of interpretation. Using an alphabet of his own making, the artist offers the visitor a world of signs and forms whose meaning escapes us, and to which he alone holds the key. In this way the visitor is led to proceed via combinatorial games and analogies to try to decipher and identify the hidden meaning of these unknown letters.

Fascinated by language's status and its modes of apparition, but at the same time no linguistic theorist, De Boeck also issues, via his alphabet, a political statement regarding illiteracy as a factor in social exclusion and rejection and the havoc it wreaks in our societies today. It is no coincidence that his close interest in the function of language and its inner codifications leads him to examine the connections between the shape of the alphabetical symbols and the aesthetics of the written that he is striving to explore. Bringing the same ease and fascination to his juggling with figures and mathematical sequences, he inventories all the combinatorial possibilities, even to the extent of devising a new subjective unit of measurement based on his own body, as *in Ldb meter #5/Knot 1* and *Ldb meter #6/Knot 2*. Once again he plays with current conventions and upsets the accepted meaning of things, but not without a touch of irony. In this he belongs to a long, fertile artistic line extending from Guy de Cointet to Marcel Broodthaers, and including, of course, Marcel Duchamp. Backed up by these aesthetic affinities and his own formal and conceptual manoeuvrings, he offers us exhibitions which, in testimony to his freedom of spirit, subvert current practice and seek to emancipate us temporarily from the standardised worlds that permanently confront us.

How to breathe new life into the exhibition experience? What's the social role of the artist today? What part should the museum be playing in our contemporary crisis-ridden societies?

These questions lie at the heart of Lieven De Boeck's artistic agenda; they have a special relevance today and must mobilise the art community towards affirmation of its convictions, assertion of its right to speak freely, and emancipation from all conventions that offer no window onto the future. *Post No Bills*, okay, but let's learn to look beyond appearances.

Image Not Found

During a residency in Los Angeles, Lieven De Boeck was struck by the cloudless blue of the Southern California sky, so clear and luminous that it begged to be reached out and touched. Yet air is transparent, immaterial, incapable of being grasped by hand unless captured in a photograph (inevitably distorting the intensity of the colour and corrupting the intended message). *Image Not Found* is De Boeck's reckoning with L.A., his investigation into light and air, into presence and absence: a non-linear search for an explanation to the childhood question "why is the sky blue?"

    We often say "blue sky thinking" to mean that we should imagine without limits, ignore conventional boundaries, and chance the miscommunication that art typically strives to avoid. This is one reason artists go on retreats (for instance to L.A.), leaving familiar spaces hoping their thinking will likewise unleash itself. However, in the digital age that same deep blue is also a colour of disruption. When a computer crashes, or there is a lack of communication between video equipment, rather than a flashing red screen the result is a stark blue field with the text "image not found" — a deep irony for those whose job is to communicate through images. For De Boeck, this blue is a default code for blank slate, tabula rasa, start over and try again.

    One version of *Image Not Found* is presented in the decidedly mid-century medium of a slide projector (itself a technical precursor to the video monitor). But unlike a typical slide show, De Boeck's projector does not cycle and click. It gives us an unchanging picture materialized on a blank wall, a wall without which the static light, i.e. the image, would dissolve into nothing (and be "not found").

    The second version of Image Not Found goes one step further by removing the referential blue sky altogether. Instead, De Boeck presents a mirror silkscreened with just the text. A "through the looking glass" destabilization of form and function — and, once again, of medium and message — that would be immediately recognized by Wonderland's Alice. While a slide projector depends on light shining from behind to articulate its image, mirrors depend on light reflecting off their polished surfaces for effect, as well as the subjective angle of the viewer's eye as the final arbiter of the mirror's contents (which also places us in danger of not "finding" the "image" if we approach it the wrong way).

Image Not Found, 2011
Slide, projector

Puzzle: Image Not Found

The formal categories of the De Boeck's *White Flags* – abstract shapes, crosses, stars, moons, circles, and figures – are also the bases for the letters of his individuated New York alphabet. For this project, the artist completed a walk through New York City, taking pictures of spray paint graffiti and other impromptu mementos of the streets that could be seen as formal derivatives of these same categories. These pictures in turn became the references for the New York Alphabet, with the first picture as letter A and the twenty-sixth picture becoming letter Z. These letters were then developed into a usable font so that De Boeck had, in the end, created his own alphabet. However, this is an alphabet that exasperated the historical identity of the letters we use everyday, stretching out their integrity as recognizable and universal forms and replacing/replicating them through an official looking, but completely arbitrary, system.

    The title of the show the *Alphabet* appeared in, *image not found*, is thus translated into an individual's alphabet and represented in a puzzle consisting of thirteen models which are intended to function as different conceptual lenses, decoder keys really, for examining the artist's own artistic studies. Some of these models are realized in a 1/1 scale within the exhibition, while others are replicated in various sizes (as if viewed through a mirror from a distance).

    As every letter is an object on a stand, a model, or an art piece itself, they attempt to visually explain the codes, the ideas, the forms, and also the media employed in De Boeck's practice. It is a conceptual catalogue of possibilities, a montage of the reading, observing, and feeling that occurs in an artist's studio, life, and gallery. They are a landscape composed entirely of coulisses, a chessboard of miscellany that reveals different ways of visiting (much like Alice), of presenting nonlinear or oblique ways of looking at the world around us.

Opposite and next spread:
Puzzle, Image Not Found (detail and overview), 2016
Variable materials
Variable dimensions

Letter I

The letter I appears as a wall made out of wax blocks (which are, in fact, a step in the process of making the colored crystal blocks found elsewhere in the original exhibition). These wax blocks are tagged with the letter I as an appropriation of "trademarking", which also acts here as a signature as well as a cipher, three basic approaches that permeate De Boeck's practice. The malleability and lack of permanence of a wax, it also suggests an undermining of the stability of the self, the "I" in which so much time, energy, and meaning is invested.

Letter I 1/20 (Tag), 2016
IKB paint on wax blocks
40 × 40 × 8 cm

Letter M

The letter M, emerges like a sign used for the Metro or McDonald's and is sculpted in neon lighting. Neon is a medium De Boeck often uses, and these neon works are generally text-based. Here, however, by translating the letter M into the artist's own alphabet, it loses its sense as a piece of writing and becomes an image only. As the irregular shape cannot be produced in classic neon, it instead becomes a blown glass sculpture.

Letter M 1/1, 2016
Neon
21 × 30 cm

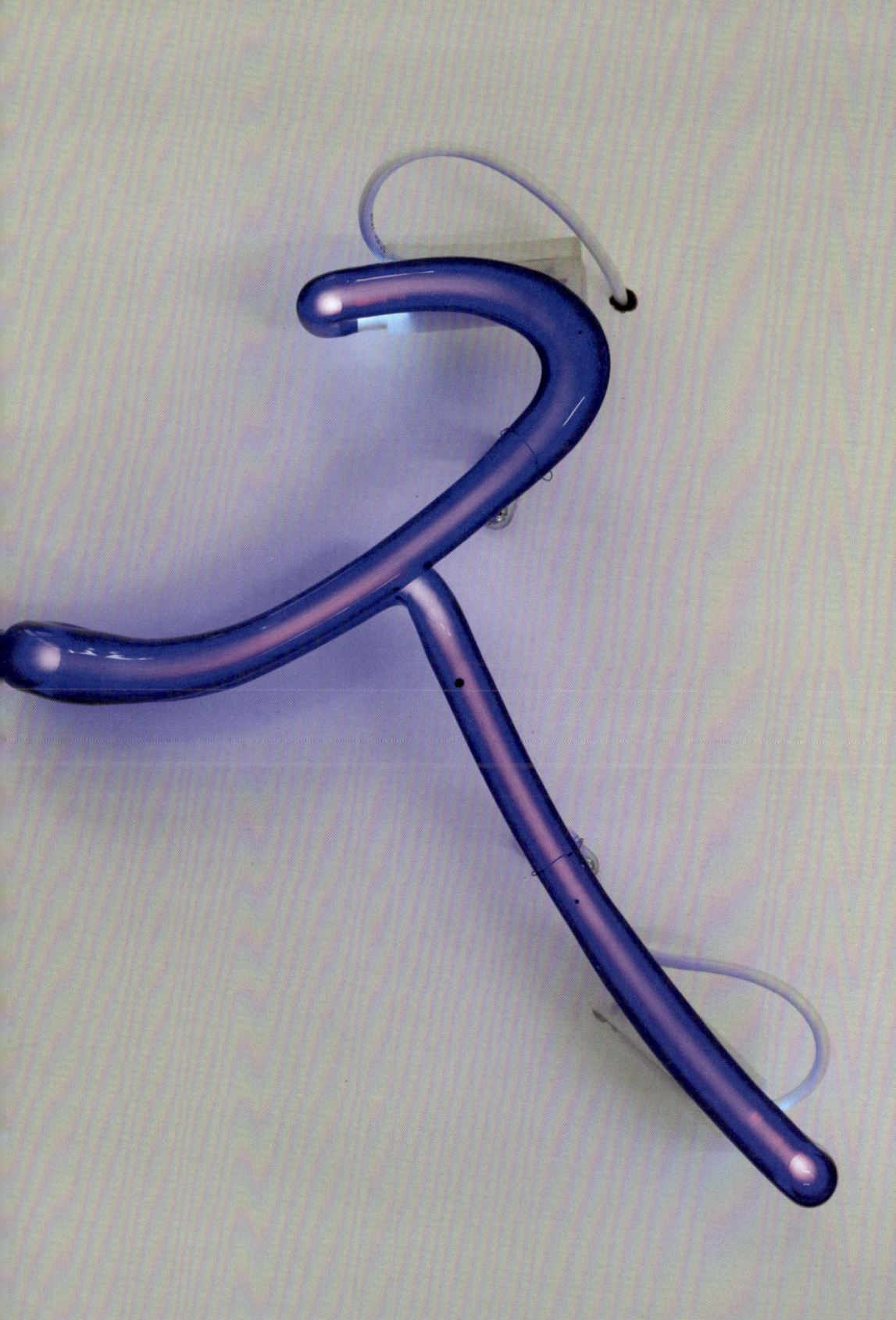

Letter A

The letter A exists as a negative space in between four socles made out of Styrofoam. The letter A of the NY Alphabet has the shape of an irregular ring shape. The cut-out form in the Styrofoam is based on the Bicycle Wheel sculpture of Marcel Duchamp, it is an exact cutout replica in the Styrofoam, but then the wheel itself is altered by the letter A, which is an irregular wheel-like shape – all the references seem to say "similar to, but not the same." The work can never exist fully on its own, but only in between this collage of similarities, thus it may be completed within the visitor's imagination. Like a 3-D puzzle, the abstract forms can be held together inside one's head in order to apprehend the total image. Consequently, the *objet trouvé* here has been replaced by a kind of *surface trouvé* translated into a three-dimensional shape, the image being recognizable as "real" yet also not able to exist in the physical space of the gallery.

Letter A 1/1 (After Duchamp), 2016
Polystyrene
(4 ×) 45 × 45 × 150 cm

Letter G

The letter G appears through a series of condensations and so is an interpretation of the 1965 *Condensation Cube* of Hans Haacke. The condensation cube here sets in play a rather complex game of illusions between the museum and the architecture that defines its space. This revolves not only around the word "cube" (galleries being often being reduced to "white cubes"), but also around the status of condensation as a *cultural* as opposed to *physical* or *natural* construct. While the appearance not only of the letter G, but also of two moons and a dot, helps manifest the idea of an irregular mirror, a phantom image, perhaps the entire universe, they also, in a straightforward sense, provide a "front" to the cube.

Letter G 1/1 (Condensation Cube), 2016
Water, plexi
40 × 40 × 40 cm

Letter E

The letter E is a model of the star plinth that appears elsewhere in the gallery. Cast in black concrete, this model attracts us through its intense, almost glossy materiality and density, while the "real" version is in fact made in hard foam – solid, but surprisingly light.

Letter E 1/5 (Scultura Vivente), 2016
Black polished concrete, messing
20 × 20 × 45 cm

Letter E

The letter E is a plinth in the form of a star, I subtitle it with *scultura vivente* (or "living sculpture" a reference to mid-century Italian art market ironist Piero Manzoni's 1961 work). The plinth invites every visitor to themselves become an art piece on display for a few minutes, to experience his or her Warholian 15 minutes of fame.

Letter E 1/1 (Scultura Vivente), 2016
EPS
50 × 130 cm

Letter N 1/1 Light Beam

After the plinth, visitors find a blue spotlight (the letter N). This is a translation of the idea of the plinth to the world of the theater, where the actor is foregrounded by lighting effects, and operates as a "living" mirror reflecting our world. Echoing further the letter E, when an actor or performer is honored for their accomplishments and contributions, they receive a star in the Walk of Fame, with their identity is presented/preserved by the written name.

Letter N 1/1 (Light Beam), 2016
Light projection
Dimensions variable

Letter O 1/1 O2O

Letter O is a huge banner obstructing the visitor's path, a reference to Daniel Buren's monumental 2005 installation *Peinture-Sculpture* in the famous rotunda of the Guggenheim Museum in New York. Here, the flag is divided into stripes that reveal the mathematical series of Fibonnacci (1, 1, 2, 3, 5, 8), which is the basis for the Golden Ratio and as such is considered as the foundational equation for beauty in art or nature. The rule of beauty itself appears in the exhibition with two of my letter O (or rather, "oo"). The meaning of oo can be interpreted in many ways: as a sound when one is awed by something beautiful ("Oh!"), or surprised by a twist in logic, or the experience of disappointment or dissatisfaction ("Oh."), or even like Fibonacci unfolding into the symbol for infinity (∞) – but without the sound, the letter(s) may convey all these emotions and ideas at once

Letter O 1/1 (O to O) (detail), 2016
Nylon, tulle, embroidery
200 × 500 cm

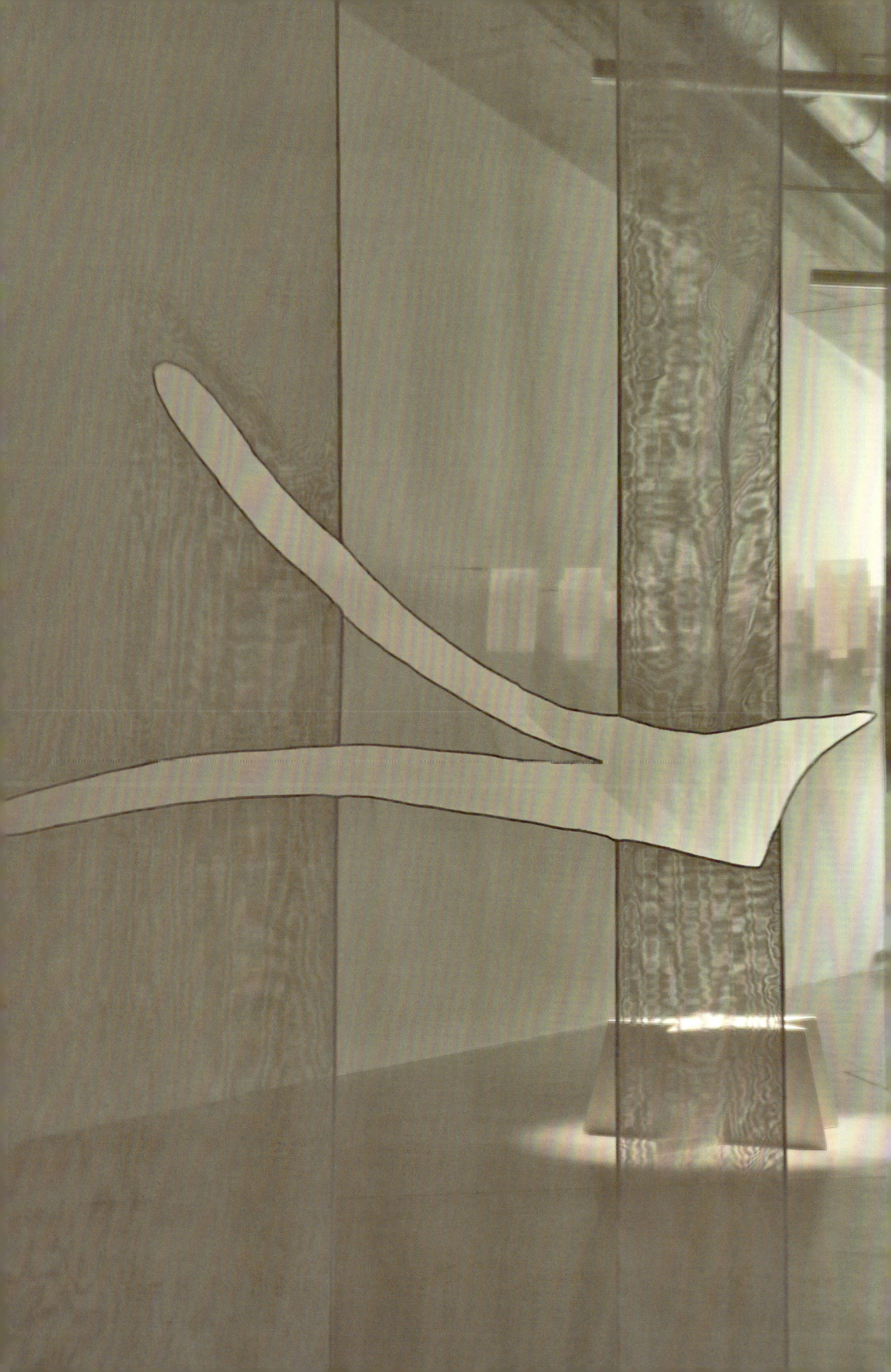

Letter T

The next letter is T is a leftover of a poured polyester plate, a "shadow" of the artist's purposeful activity. Once again, the materiality and the remnants of the art-making process refer directly to De Boeck's own practice as itself the subject of inquiry.

Letter T 1/1, 2016
Acryl glass in metal frame
80 × 200 cm

Found

Then, the letter F, formed as a drawing by a red-gloved finger through a field of white sand (used to make glass) – the disaster of the sand's purity being spoiled creates a shape in negative space. It is a child's drawing on the beach, simple, yet fully aware of its own impending erasure by wave or wind, its creation pregnant with its destruction.

Follows a second letter O, here as a banner modeled in scale after the full-size banner.

The letter U is a model for a sculpture, here made in ceramics.

The letter N is based on a work called *The Parrot*, (*Le Perroquet*), which is a chessboard of image slides on a lightbox. The white slides contain drawings and writings that are all references to existing artworks that were interpreted by the artist in order to literally highlight ways of working as an artist. However, the interpretations operate as copies of the original, and so, as above, imply the meaningless repetition of a parrot, a repetition that has now tellingly become part of a serious art practice.

The letter D is a model of a work affectionately called *perfect lovers*, with a part of the letter made out of Ice, while the other is a candle. They form material opposites, but also suggest inherent similarities for as one disappears so does the other (a gesture towards Felix Gonzalez-Torres time-sensitive displays that were not meant to endure past their exhibition).

Puzzle, Image Not Found, 2016
Variable materials
Variable dimensions

Le Perroquet

Le Perroquet is a chessboard of slides arranged on a lightbox. The black slides are empty while the white ones contain drawings and texts, photos of elements that inspire De Boeck and that relate to his discourse as an artist. Every time it is presented, an element is added or rearranged to suggest both the repetition inherent in making art, as well as the sense of originality that does in fact emerge from this repetition. Hence, the title of the work *Le Perroquet* or parrot, as the actions undertaken are copies of images or documents that transfer surfaces without also transferring real meaning or understanding.

Le Perroquet, 2010
Light box with 64 slides
44 × 44 × 21 cm

Autoportrait contre Nature

The *auto portrait contre nature* – a "self-portrait against nature" that is intended as an image of imageless-ness – presents the abstract idea of light itself as an image or a portrait, suggested by the slide placed in portrait format in an old-fashioned carousel.
   The work in this way introduces a reflection of the viewer looking through a "peephole" at the portrait slide: a mirrorless reflection of action and conscious effort rendered as an "image" of pure light.
   The *auto portrait contre nature* has several different presentation formats. Sometimes it is projected on an empty piece of letter paper, inviting viewers to consider the light as creating a kind of written portrait. Sometimes it is visible through a peephole, drawing a connection with the scandalous étant donné of Marcel Duchamp, the work this persistent interrogator of artistic legibility constructed in secret and was only discovered after his death: an unexpected return to the figurative as well as a *clinq d'oeuil* towards the lusty reality of Courbet.

Autoportrait contre Nature (detail), 2009
Slide, slide projector, letter paper (# 02)
Variable dimensions
Collection Gensollen, La Fabrique, Marseille

Autoportrait contre Nature (detail), 2009

Andre Gordts

Kaleidoscope Kaleidoscope Kaleidoscope Kaleidoscope Kaleidoscope Kaleidoscope Kaleidoscope Kaleidoscope Kaleidoscope Kaleidoscope Kaleidoscope

"L'artiste n'est pas seul à accomplir l'acte de création car le spectateur établit le contact de l'œuvre avec le monde extérieur en déchiffrant et en interprétant ses qualifications profondes et par là ajoute sa propre contribution au processus créatif." (Marcel Duchamp)

"... mais je me sens bien plus à l'aise à la foire de Cologne que dans mon propre Musée, car sur le Kunstmarkt nous nous trouvons en plein dans la réalité de la société contemporaine, au beau milieu de son système, qui se révèle être bassement commercial. Parce que c'est la vie de chacun, l'existence de pratiquement tous les artistes, les directeurs de musée et des galléries. Bassement commerciale – je ne veux pas dire que tous ces gens sont odieux, ou vils, mais que l'art est vendu là comme une marchandise méprisable." (Marcel Broodthaers)

Asked to organise the accrochage of the first exhibition of the Society of Independent Artists in 1917 at Grand Central Palace in New York, Marcel Duchamp presented the works by alphabetical order of the artists' names, creating an impression which can be approximated to the overwhelming situation of a contemporary art fair. It made Duchamp the godfather of this kind of event, contrasting sharply with his own work and being very careful of the collectors he wanted to place his work with. This in-between relationship of the artist with the collector is the Scylla and Charybdis every artist has to circumnavigate, carefully (or less-carefully) creating a work in his or her head; planning it in the studio; materialising it, alone or with the help of skilled professionals; cherishing the work until it leaves the factory or the workshop – and then it disappears, escaping control of its maker, leaving for a gallery, bought by a museum or a collector, used by a curator in an exhibition, with or without the artist's consent. The work gets a life of its own which is not always easy: *"The handling and preservation in a museum, which is expected to be careful, is often careless. Sometimes the staff seems to resent the art. Usually the view is that the damage done doesn't matter and can be repaired. Even with the best intentions of a director or curator the installation is seldom good because the rooms are not. Always of course the exhibitions are temporary. Finally, the artist lends work, accepts damage to it – insurance is a joke – gives time, and gets next to nothing: "The work is out in the public". The artist should be paid for a public exhibition as everyone is for a public activity."* (Donald Judd, 1982).

    Foremost, once it has left the studio, the work of a given artist lives on in his or her head, documented in a kind of *Boîte-en-Valise*, dialoguing with the other works of the *oeuvre*. Here it lives an immaterial life, but a life that makes sense as it is related to the rest of the production. At the other end of the chain, the collector who bought one (or more) works of the artist is supposed to be the guard of this work: buying a piece of art is not a gratuitous act. It means the collector carries part of the responsibility of preserving the work and, as Duchamp writes, of interpreting its deeper qualifications and contributing to the creative process in a one-on-one relationship, which is widened to anyone who sees it when the work is lent for an exhibition. For a work is fragile, as Judd rightly states. So the acquisition of a work is not just a financial transaction, but also a transaction of responsibility.

The problem of sustaining the life of an artwork once it has been included in a collection, be it a museum or a private collection, is not a simple one. The many layers embedded in the work can only exist through (preferably permanent) dialogue, which is usually nothing more than a distant fata morgana. Lieven De Boeck tried to offer a solution during his exhibition *Image not Found* at the FRAC PACA in Marseille by staging a performance act that was leading the audience through the exhibition.

He offered a possible read of the exhibition as a work of art by creating a *parcours* through this real *musée imaginaire*, consciously introducing the lapse of *time* as the performers lead the way for the audience, walking from one piece to another, reading the words of the *Hollywood Alphabet*, manipulating the *Lego blocks* and glass *mikado* bars in a playful but serious way. Evolving with the performers through the exhibition, the public in fact was offered an image of itself: exhibition of the work and exposition of the audience through its reflection in a mirror, which could be a lie. Or not. Identifying reflections of identities, reflecting visitors, reflecting about the exhibition as a language rebus in which the signs of the alphabet have been emptied of their standard meaning, and replaced by other signs only to be read through the meaning given by the artist. The meaning of the artist manipulates the meaning of the work and the reading of the exhibition. In fact, the artist is the architect of meaning by rejecting the standardised interpretation of his measuring tools, creating a gap with what is currently accepted *as the truth*, for example the length of a meter, modulating this *certainty* with the knowledge of the past.

Dislocation of language, of signs, of meaning, of place, of colour. Emptying national flags of their colour deprives them of their identity, literally dislocates them through a typological non-alphabetical grid, replacing their country names by their geometrical abstract symbols.

Communication: undercutting written language using units called *letters* to form words, a system which took thousands of years to develop and refine, that gives us the advantage of communication, to arrange our thoughts but also our bookkeeping and our control over the world. A very fine generalised system. Why not use this general classification for personal purposes? Overlaying the known units with a layer of homemade signs, transforming messages into rebuses, as Marcel Broodthaers did on his tombstone. The artist as an interpreter putting us on the wrong track. But is it the wrong track we are trying to decipher? Puzzling.

The artist's view is at least original. Or is it not? The artist replicates known objects as in *La série bleu*. Evidently Lego blocks. But are they? Tricky business… In childhood most of us played with Lego, constructing worlds by clicking blocks together, forming houses that remain somewhere in our memories… But are we looking at the original Lego? Is it a replica? A repetition? Or perhaps a ready-made? It is made out of glass, the artist painstakingly created something totally different from the idea we have of this block, in the same way Robert Gober created his *Drain* pieces. These are artworks, made by skilled technicians, loaded with a meaning we do not comprehend at first sight. They are not copies of the *original* and not even replicas as they answer to the mathematical laws of Fibonacci. True, they were made with the technique of the mould, *moule* in French, evidently referring to Marcel Broodthaerts' mussels and to Marcel Duchamp's *Moules Mâlic*. The social and political moulds through which we are all modelled, without knowing even it. *Etant donné*.

Blue. Blue light. Neon light. A medium quite often employed by the artist. An homage to IKB Yves Klein. Really? The blue used as background in the film and television industry to project images on the screen, the ever-present blue, not shown to the audience; the internal kitchen of mass-communication, an excellent passe-partout to manipulate the final image. The perfect visual lies. And did we eventually find the unfound image?

Défence d'afficher: it is forbidden to accept ready-made opinions. *On ne s'affiche point*.

La Boîte en valise belge (detail), 2009
Various materials
42 × 44 × 15 cm

La Boîte en valise belge

Another art historical concept that explored the status of the museum is the *boîte en valise* of Marcel Duchamp. At the Getty Institute in Los Angeles, the artist was allowed a personal viewing of one of Duchamp's boxes, conceived as kind of portable museum. Following this encounter, De Boeck created an exact copy in plastic in the colors of the Belgian Flag, containing a miniaturized copy of the various elements and artworks that make up the "Belgian section" of his artistic output. This miniaturization into plastic is also a reference to the inherent duplicity of the material, and so of art in general: plastic of course being the most expedient method of casting, a sign of the modern age, its ability to cheaply replicate and hence a mark of its disposability, and in this way the very opposite of a museum's status as a guardian of the rare and precious. Yet De Boeck's *Valise* is likewise curated and full of personally significant objects with their own value far apart from the mere use value their common material might imply. In the end, as perhaps the artist suggests, we're all carrying around richly endowed museums in our bags.

Explorations, 2016
Performance, video still

Musée d'Art Moderne – Archives des aigles disparus

The work is comprised of 41 eagles cut out of letter paper and framed. Every eagle represents a kind of identity, like a heraldic sign, a family crest, or perhaps an airfreight company, or even a country's emblem, the insignia of a city, etc. The work is also intended to immediately engage in a dialogue with the work of Marcel Broodthaers and his *musée d'art modern, department des aigles*.

For several years De Boeck has been working on a body of work that unfolds itself as a personal archive, *The Archive of Disappearance* (2010-present). *The Archive of Disappearance* is a research project into what a purely *typological* exhibition would be – of which the eagle artworks are one branch of study. This research is thus posed as a question, one that challenges the museum's space and its codified functions by closely examining the *status* of a work of art and its related typologies – be they formal, stylistic or conceptual. *The Archive of Disappearance* is expressed elsewhere by the Golden Ratio, classic canons of beauty, notions of originality, integer sequences (Fibonacci numbers), units of measurement and various architectural vocabularies, and here through copy and archetype as well as the readymade. These form the territories of research, producing an object series that is both highly visual and broadly conceptual, as absorbing to audiences as a puzzle and as open-ended as a paradox: a bird taking flight.

Musée d'Art Moderne – Archives des aigles disparus, 2010
41 cut-out sheets of paper
31 × 22.3 cm (framed)
Collection F. Rouvez, Brussels

Next spread:
RÉBUS #1, 2012
Mirror, vinyl, polystyrene, wood
4 panels of 60.5 × 43 × 6 cm and 2 panels of 60.5 × 123 × 6cm

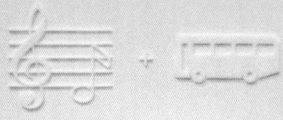

POUR LIRE LA SOLUTION, RENVERSEZ L'IMAGE

POUR LIRE LA SOLUTION, RENVERSEZ L'IMAGE

Série Bleue

For *Série Bleue*, Lieven De Boeck collaborated with a research centre on glass CIRVA in the South of France to create a series of Lego-like blocks in a nostalgic, vitreous blue at once as luscious as candy and as cold and brittle as the most delicate crystal glass. While the crafting of the bricks was complicated and highly technical – involving the laser-printing of the cast to excise any logos – the idea behind their development was that of a return to basics, to a lack of pre-defined images, to the literal building blocks of an identity.

The various glass bricks were serialized and scaled according to a Fibonacci sequence (1, 1, 2, 3, and 5), which has its origins in the Golden Section found across natural ratios that form the stylistic basis for harmonious compositions in art, architecture, and music. The presentation of the scaled iterations, in turn, each express a fragment from the artist, his work and life, but never reveal his complete self.

The smallest series, "Scale 1", is placed in a circle around a print of De Boeck's iris reflecting his studio window (the eye, of course, being an age-old "window" into the soul, a portal between inside and outside). A second "Scale 1" is an arrangement in which the distance between the blocks conforms to a Fibonacci sequence, with each space of separation scaled to the artist's thumbprint in blue ink – the state's measure of a man and a criminal's I.D, but also a gesture towards the child's carefree desire to finger the blocks and leave sticky traces behind. The interplay between print and block indicates that perhaps the glass piece is itself the best way to know De Boeck.

"Scale 2", while looking haphazard, is in fact organized along the lines of De Boeck's enlarged initials "LDB," whited-out with Tipp-Ex. The blocks define the letters volumetrically rather than linearly, indicating that a signature – unlike an eye-colour or a fingerprint – is designed by the artist himself, and moulded over a lifetime. The blanked signature also invokes the seminal 16 mm film by fellow Belgian artist Marcel Broodthaers, Une seconde d'éternité, during which Broodthaers wrote his initials "MB" in one second. Whether initials (or a signature) can stand in for the eternal, here they capture an extrinsic aspect of a self, the longing for permanence residing in shared memory, time, community, and, less often, artistic celebrity.

"Scale 3" is positioned on a white Belgian flag. The white flag is not a symbol of indifference to the artist's nationality and the location of his artistic practice, but a reference to a much earlier work based on a sequence of world-wide flags all executed in white, denuding them of their specificity and ascribing them with a post-Cold War sameness. In this way, the white flag is a "surrender" to the forces of globalization that has drained individuality from regional identities, leaving only an allegiance to technical and technological conformity as possibilities for self-understanding. Hence the preciousness of De Boeck's hand-crafted blocks, logo-free but associated with the "official" categories of corporate trademark and biometric data: eye-scans, fingerprints, signatures – are a measure of ourselves that is at once universal and arbitrary.

Scale 5" takes up the work of measuring the self, instigated by "Scale 1." Unlike the previous scales, "Scale 5" blocks are not preserved in a showcase, but exposed: they are meant to be handled, their weight should surprise, the effort of grasping an individual, his identity, should be work, should carry the weight of real bricks rather than ethereal glass. Here, De Boeck himself functions as the "meter" along which the blocks are laid out. His own measurements coordinate the blocks according to a prearranged, yet self-chosen gauge. It is both architectural – a brick after all builds a building – and a deeply personalized quasi-portrait, giving us a sense of De Boeck's own size, his own ability to take up the space around us, without ever actually showing us his "looks." He remains imageless, but somehow fully material.

The various scales allow childhood toys to crystalize into usable images of the self, a made-to-measure matrix that drafts the conventions of identity imposed by schools, governments, offices – even our parentage – and reorders them according to our own internal desires. Ultimately, the subject of Série Bleue is both Lieven De Boeck the artist and how De Boeck fits into the world: neatly, like one toy brick clicked into place; awkwardly, like a fragile bloom of hand-cast glass.

Next spread:
Série Bleue (detail), 2014
25 bricks in blue Crystal glass, paper, ink on paper, silk, ink, Tipp-Ex
Variable dimensions
Production in collaboration with CIRVA
Collection Féraud / Fonds M-ARCO

Série Bleue (detail), 2014

Série Bleue (detail), 2014

Série Bleue (detail), 2014

Série Bleue (detail), 2014

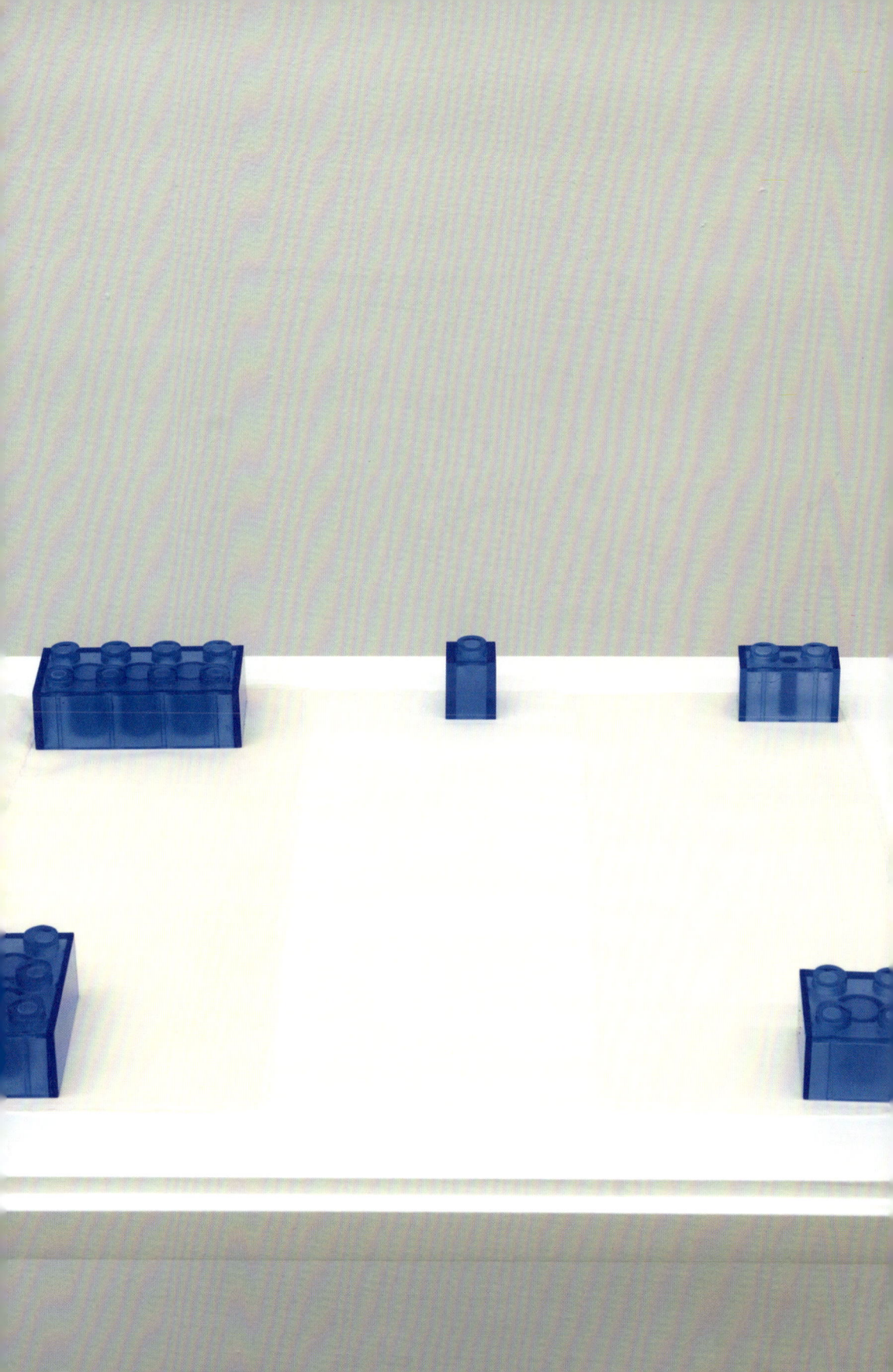

I lie

The neon light piece *I lie* presents a candid phrase that is assertive and outwardly honest, while undermining the very notion of honesty: in artistic representation, in authorship (indeed it is the beginning of the artist's name *Lie*-ven), in the publicity that undergirds these endeavors, and in the idea of the mirror as a teller of truth. The paradox of this lie is that it is registered as a sign for all to see: what value is there in hiding or shielding the truth with a lie, when the lie itself is so exposed?

I lie, 2012
Neon
18 × 15 cm

Five Rings, Found-transported-restored and Hanging, 2016
5 circular neons, Ø 39 cm
Variable dimensions

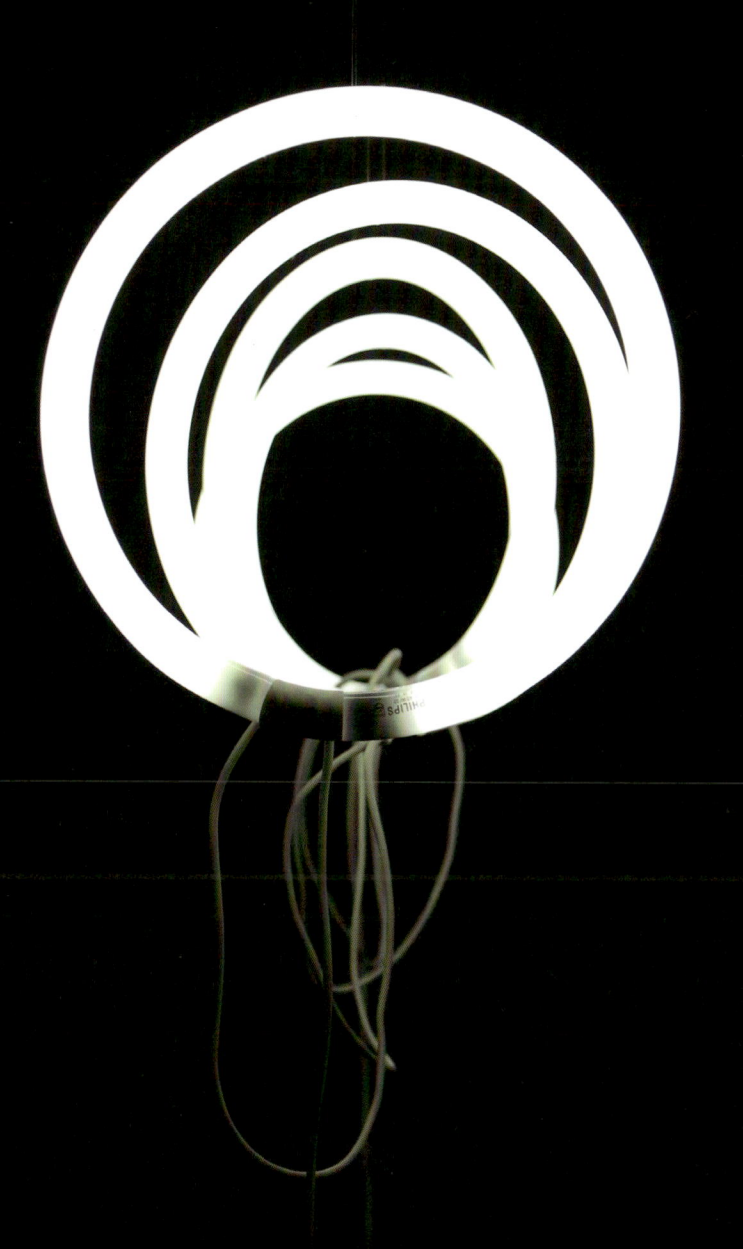

Five Rings, Found-transported-restored and Hanging, 2016

Artist's Biography

Lieven De Boeck

For several years, Lieven De Boeck (BE, 1971) has been working on an oeuvre that unfolds as a personal archive in which he incorporates various classifications and typologies. In his work, De Boeck plays with mirrorings, distortions and connections, through which he creates new meanings and interpretations of identity, signs and language, the private and the public space, the original and the copy. Many of his works exist in the space between appearance and disappearance. Lieven De Boeck is represented by gallery Meessen De Clercq in Brussels.

STUDIO LDB

Founded in 2014, studio LDB is a collaborative art practice that explores the œuvre of artist Lieven De Boeck. The studio develops and shares authorship through the concepts of reproduction, re-interpretation and conceptual research on forms of presentation. In order to show hidden aspects of the work, alternative ways of making the work public are explored. Studio LDB is a currently a collaboration between Lieven De Boeck, Julia Reist and Zac Rose. The project descriptions in this book are written by Zac Rose.

www.studiolievendb.com

Authors' Biographies

After receiving a doctorate in art history devoted to Chaïm Soutine's work from the Sorbonne, **Pascal Neveux** consecutively worked at Art Public Contemporain and for the Jean Gabriel Mitterand Gallery, before joining Ivry-sur-Seine in 1992. From 1999 to 2006 he directed the Frac Alsace in Sélestat and has been in charge of the Frac Provence-Alpes-Côte d'Azur over the past ten years. President of the National Association of Fracs from 2003 to 2006 and member of the Administrative Council of Platform for ten years. He was General curator of the "Ulysses" project designed for Marseille-Provence European Cultural Capital in 2013, assembling over one hundred places and including more than 150 artists. He also writes texts and articles dedicated to numerous French and foreign artists.

Chantal Pattyn (Kortrijk, 1968) studied art history & archeology (Ghent University). In 2007 she was appointed as director of Klara (Flemish classical, jazz and culture radio) and since 2016 as manager culture at VRT (Flemish Radio & TV). She has been a radio host with a focus on art and music since 1990. Currently she is the host of the art's magazine Pompidou, broadcasted on Klara.

Jamal Mahjoub (London, 1960) is a writer of novels, short stories and essays. His work has been translated into a number of languages and has been awarded several prizes, including the Guardian African Short Story Prize, the St Malo Prix de l'Astrolabe, and the Mario Vargas Llosa Premio NH de Relatos. Since 2012 he has begun publishing crime fiction under the pen name PARKER BILAL. There are currently four books in the Cairo set series following investigator Makana.

Jannah Loontjens (1974) is a philosopher and writer. In 2007 she debuted with the novel *Good Luck*. Her second, acclaimed novel *What Time Really* (2011) was nominated for the Halewijn Literature Prize. The essay collection *My Life is Better than Literature* was published in 2013. In 2016 she published her youngest book under the title: *Roaring Nineties*, in which she combines essay, autobiography and philosophy. Loontjens teaches philosophy at ArtEZ Institute of the Arts.

André Gordts (Brussels, 1951) is a curator and artcollector specialized on the 20th and 21st Centuries. From 1993-1995 Gordts was a consultant at Sotheby's, afterwards at Christie's *Contemporary Department*, London. Since he has curated several shows and was a consultant for institutions such as Bank Brussels-Lambert, lille 3000 amongs others. André Gordts is a boardmemeber of the Museum Dhondt Dhaenens in Deurle and the Willame Foundation, Brussels.

Tanguy Eeckhout (Wilrijk, 1980) studied Art Studies and Media & Communication at Ghent University. Since 2005 he has been a member of the artistic-academic staff and active as curator at the Dhondt-Dhaenens Museum in Deurle. In recent years he has concentrated mainly on research into and presentation of both modern and contemporary art. He is also engaged in doctoral research into the significance of private collectors in Belgium in the twentieth century (at Ghent University). In addition, he regularly writes articles on modern and contemporary art.

Image Credits

Matthias Van Rossen
p 38-39, 83, 84-85, 91, 92-93, 95, 96-97, 99, 101, 113, 114-115, 118-119, 185, 187, 205

Philippe De Gobert
p 44, 48, 59, 61, 68-69, 71, 117, 121, 123, 129, 147, 175, 177, 179, 189, 190-191, 201, 202

Rik Vannevel
p 51, 52, 59, 63, 103, 104-105, 107, 125, 127, 153, 155, 156, 161, 163, 169, 173

Kristof Vrancken
p 33, 65

Maxime Boisvert
p 41, 43

Hanna Dawn
p 57, 194-195

Studio LDB
p 1, 87, 89, 109, 111, 131, 133, 171

J.C. Lette
p 3, 5, 7, 9, 11, 13, 15, 17, 19, 21, 23, 25, 27, 37, 67, 149, 150-151, 159, 165, 167, 197, 199

Karel Bruyland
p 207, 209

Photography department city of Bruges
for CC Bruges
p 34-35

Cover
New York Alphabet, 2006

Courtesy

All works are courtesy of Lieven De Boeck or Lieven De Boeck and gallery Meessen De Clercq.

Lieven De Boeck would like to thank all the curators, collectors and institutions who have supported his work through the years.

Special thanks goes to Mr et Mme Bonfils, Karima Celestin, Alexis Dragonetti, André Gordts, Hervé Lebrun, Bernadette Clot-Goudard / Martin, Carl Meeusen, Chantal Pattyn, Michèle Rollé, Frédéric Rouvez, Bernard Soens, Marc Timmermans, Fabien Van Tomme and Wivine de Traux, who financially supported this book by the acquisition of the edition *Image not Found*, specially produced for this purpose.

Onomatopee 131

X
*independence of character
- novel figures perpetrating
disappearance*
inscriptions by Lieven De Boeck

Editors: Freek Lomme, Lieven De Boeck
Authors: Andre Gordts, Chantal Pattyn, Jannah Loontjens & Jamal Mahjoub, Pascal Neveux, Tanguy Eeckhout and Zac Rose

Translators / copy editors:
John Tittensor, Mels Dees and
Nanne op t' Ende

Graphic design: Sara De Bondt with special thanks to Geoffrey Brusatto
Printing: Jeroen Bosch and Trudy Dorrepaal at Art Libro / Drukkerij Roelofs
Binding: Boekbinderij Patist

Made possible thanks to:
Museum Dhondt-Dhaenens
Frac Provence-Alpes-Côte d'Azur

Lieven De Boeck, the authors and Onomatopee © 2017

All rights reserved. No part of this publication may be reproduced, stored in a retrieval system, or transmitted in any form or by any means, electronic, mechanical, photocopying, recording or otherwise, without the prior written permission from the authors and the publisher.

www.onomatopee.net
ISBN: 978-94-91677-66-3

Published in conjunction with the following exhibitions:

Image Not Found
5 March – 5 June 2016
Frac Provence-Alpes-Côte d'Azur
www.fracpaca.org

The Fonds régional d'art contemporain (Regional Fund for Contemporary Art) is financed by the Provence-Alpes-Côte d'Azur region and the Ministry of Culture and Communication / Regional direction of cultural affairs Provence-Alpes-Côte d'Azur. It is a member of Platform, a group of Regional Funds for Contemporary Art and founding member of the Marseille Expos network.

Objet Trouvé
16 October 2016 – 15 January 2017
Museum Dhondt-Dhaenens
www.museumdd.be

The museum Dhondt-Dhaenens is a private foundation recognised by the Flemish Government. As a contemporary art centre, it aims to play an active role in the international art field.

X
10 November – 17 December 2017
Onomatopee
www.onomatopee.net

Exhibition space and publisher Onomatopee is supported by the province of Noord-Brabant. Their self-initiated program of exhibitions 2017–18 is supported by the Mondriaan Fund.